The Promised Land

The Promised Land

A life in the land of milk and honey

I perceive that we inhabitants of New England live this mean life that we do because our vision does not penetrate the surface of things. We think that is which appears to be.

— Henry David Thoreau

By: Rawls Howard

First Printing: September 2018

ISBN 978-0-578-20916-6

Copernicus Publishing
104½ East Saint James Street
Tarboro, NC 27886
Email: copernicuspublishing@gmail.com

For my wife Sue

Acknowledgements

I would like to express my deepest appreciation to Allen Proctor and all of the faculty and staff of the Haden Institute for the help and inspiration that they provided to me for the writing of this book.

Special thanks to Andy Crosland for his careful reading and insightful comments on the work as it progressed and for the amazing introduction to the book that he provided.

Victoria Kornylac. Thank you for your incredible photo composition.

Thanks also to Robin Smith for his professional expertise on the cover design.

Finally, I would also like to express my heartfelt appreciation to all of the characters in the book for the invaluable contributions you have made to my life. None of the characters in this work are fictional, however in some cases names have been changed. Additional thanks to my cousin "Joe Braswell" for his work in the surveying and mapping of The Promised Land.

The Reader

An Introduction to *The Promised Land*

Let those who want to save the world . . . see it clear and as a whole.
Ernest Hemingway
Death in the Afternoon

This "Introduction" is the result of synchronicity. It is not the consequence of a chain of cause and effect moving logically and certainly to nudge it into existence. Rather, it is born of grace or at least of a spiritual momentum that pushes people and emotions and ideas and events where it will. Explaining how this introduction came to be is perhaps the best way to begin it.

In 2006, I retired from nearly 40 years of teaching American literature to college students. In the decade that followed, I came to be a mentor in the Spiritual Direction Program of the Haden Institute in North Carolina. A mentor is assigned to a group of students. He or she reads their essays and reflections, comments, answers their questions, and provides the group with leadership and support. In March of 2017, Rawls Howard—the author of this book—began studies at Haden, and I became his mentor.

As readers of these pages will soon see, Rawls—aka Adam— fearlessly marches to the beat of his own drum. He had no interest in becoming a spiritual director. Allen Proctor, Director of the Haden Institute, agreed to work with Rawls and me to develop a special course of study to foster Rawls' personal and spiritual development. That soon took the shape of Rawls writing *The Promised Land* while he participated in the Haden offerings and activities. Rawls, who has written other books, again became an author, and I again became a reader. Thus began a rich and enlightening journey for both of us—one neither of us had anticipated or sought.

Students at Haden are asked to write reflections on books they read and essays that show their understanding of key aspects of their training. As a mentor, I usually try to echo what they say and to comment on points I find interesting or important. This interchange is not a literary exercise, so it is quite different from the explications and analyses that were the backbone of my research and teaching in academia. Rawls and his new program of study suddenly took me back to familiar ground. Once again, I focused on plot, character, figurative language, point of view and other facets of literary criticism. It was an unexpected gift.

However, I was at Haden to be a mentor, and Rawls was there for spiritual growth. No matter how enjoyable our new prospects were, we had work to do. Had we really found a way to do it?

I'd like to think so. As you read this autobiographical novel, you will see Adam's life and understanding unfold. Adam's creator unflinchingly marches his character through many hellish moments. As Adam matures, he tries to understand the meaning of these and other experiences. Thus, the novel becomes a venue for Rawls to make sense of his own spiritual journey—to seek the import of his life.

Spiritual direction occurs when a director works with a person to help foster growth, insight, and change. The director is more a catalyst in this process than an agent. He or she does not teach or lead but creates a safe and sacred space where the client, relying on the Spirit for guidance, finds the way.

Although my relation to Rawls was not meant to be spiritual direction, our experience was similar to it in at least one way. The novel became our safe and sacred space. Writing in the first person, Rawls used the character Adam to examine his past. Using the persona of literary critic, I commented on the meanings and motifs that I saw in the work and therefore in Rawls' past. In that role, I attempted to offer a little water to help nurture the spiritual growth that was taking place for the author. Unlike the Victorian readers whose reactions shaped the serial novels of Dickens and Thackeray, I had no influence on the direction of this book. But I do like to think I might have done a little to encourage the author by helping maintain and light the safe and sacred space of his creation.

The important thing about this work for most readers is that it is more than an exercise in navel gazing by its author. This is a serious novel—one to which we can apply the standard paraphernalia of literary criticism. It is a cliché in "spiritual" circles that the activity of creation is more important than its product. Well, this is a product that matters. It deserves and commands the readers' attention.

Casual readers who just want a good story will find *The Promised Land* to be a page-turner. Students of character can savor Adam as he grows and changes throughout his life. Close readers will discern symbols and recurrent motifs as young Adam shoots guns and sets off explosives as his inner child blows away. They will find him speeding down the Interstates in mid-career while his life is zooming out of control. When Adam begins to soar spiritually, he pilots small planes through the skies, sometimes putting his faith in instruments when he must fly blindly. Finally, Adam reconstructs himself just as he rebuilds a new home from the flotsam and jetsam of this old career.

Although *The Promised Land* is an autobiographical search for self, it deals with some interesting larger notions. Adam in this novel—like Gatsby, Billy Budd, Holden Caulfield, and many others before him—is the "American Adam in the New World Garden." He is an innocent born into a land of opportunity that is haunted by an alluring and corrupting materialism. Dazzled by the cars, the drinks, the lovers, the money, the stuff, the very excitement of America, he is also drawn to its idealism and values and Spirit. He is, in short, another battleground in this particularly American war.

Adam also is a very masculine character. Masculinity, here, is not to be equated with gender. In Adam's America, it involves such qualities as strength, courage, independence, violence, and assertiveness. A man is measured by his paycheck. He is inclined to squelch his femininity—his caring, gentleness, empathy, and compassion. Because masculinity is closely associated with the patriarchal, it is more often questioned than admired.

Adam hunts, drives fast cars, womanizes, can sometimes be violent and aggressive, makes a lot of money, and goes his own way. He is a study in masculinity—even becoming the archetype of the wise old man by the end of the novel. Such characters are scarce now, and this novel is unusual in its unshrinking portrayal of a masculine man who is not of the scrubbed, acceptable variety described by sociologist Irving Goffman as "a young, married, white, urban, northern, heterosexual Protestant father of college education, fully employed, of good complexion, weight and height, and a recent record in sports." Adam emerges as strongly masculine in his vices and virtues, his charisma and his warts, his strengths and his weaknesses, his victories and his defeats.

In addition to his defining Americanness and masculinity, Adam also is very much a Southerner. He lives in a small town, and he is keenly aware of social class. He's involved in AA, family dynamics, technology, business, and church. He is rich and he is poor. Adam's experiences raise various theological and philosophical issues. In other words, *The Promised Land* presents a rich literary landscape for readers to explore. What you discover here depends partly on what you bring with you and partly on what you are looking for. But any reader can be confident of finding something arresting in these pages.

Andy Crosland
Spartanburg, SC
2018

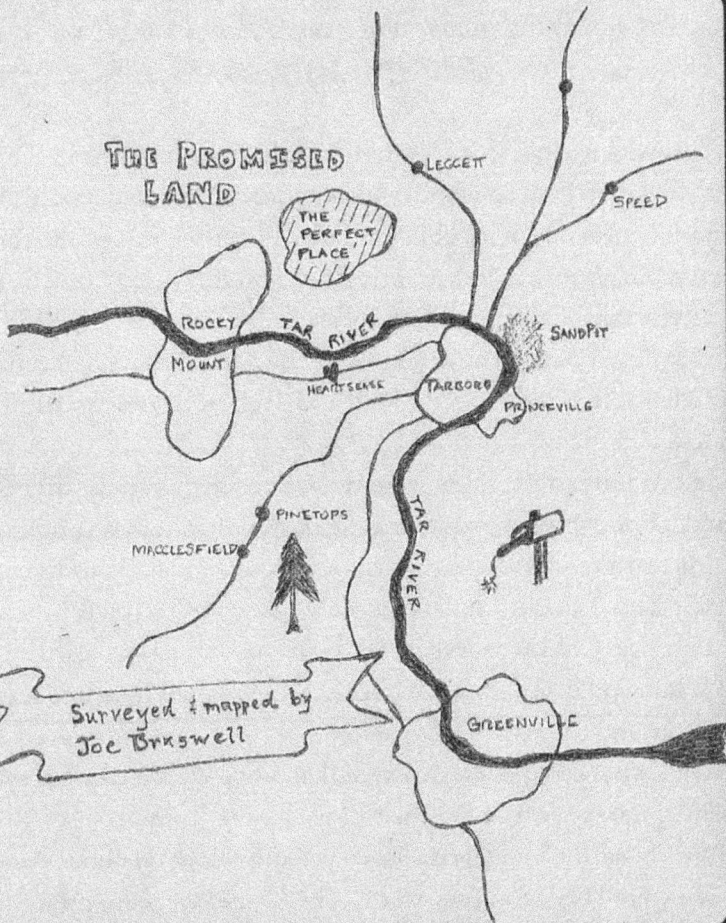

THE PROMISED LAND

'THE PERFECT PLACE'

LEGGETT

SPEED

ROCKY MOUNT

TAR RIVER

SANDPIT

HEARTSEASE

TARBORO

PRINCEVILLE

TAR RIVER

PINETOPS

MACCLESFIELD

Surveyed & mapped by
Joe Braswell

GREENVILLE

Foreword

In the Beginning

Certainly Adam in Paradise had not more sweet and curious apprehensions of the world than I when I was a child. — Thomas Traherne

Growing up in a small Eastern North Carolina town in the mid-twentieth century was a wonderful experience. We had a very "Mark Twainish" existence, with children being given the run of the town. We took our shoes off in the springtime and they pretty much stayed off (except for Sunday) until school started.

We played outside after supper in the summertime, collecting jars full of "lightnin bugs", playing hide-and-seek, and going to the Town Pool to swim.

In our little town, there were two policemen on duty after 5:00 pm and, although there was some serious crime, there was none of the sense of fear that is so pervasive in our society today. Our house was generally kept unlocked unless we were going out of town overnight.

True, the Cold War was in full swing and when the alarm at the Town Hall would sound, we school children would hide under our desks from the Russians. But we felt that they were far away. Of course we were completely unaware that while we were doing this, the Russian children were under their desks hiding from us.

We "liked Ike", pledged allegiance, and felt good about America.

We were "US" and they were "Them" and we were pretty sure that "They" were nothing to worry about because we were manly and tough. Like Davey Crockett and John Wayne.

I was a white male who was born into a privileged family. This put me at the top of America's unacknowledged caste system. When I looked around me there was (once again) "Us" and there was everyone else. Another Us and another Them. And once again it was of the utmost importance to know that we were much better (smarter, richer, more sophisticated, and so on) than Them. It made life safe and made sleeping at night with "sweet dreams" possible.

Before the advent of the ethnic diversity that we enjoy today (and I for one, really do enjoy it) our population was, quite literally, black and white. There was a street in our town, Panola Street, which divided the two communities. East of Panola Street the population was black. West of Panola Street, the population was white. East was East, and West was West, and never the twain should meet.

My parents were elegant people. My father had been born at the end of the 19th Century into a situation that was, quite literally, right out of *Gone with the Wind*. There was an enormous house, called by our family "the big house". Servants were everywhere, and mahogany and silver were present in staggering abundance.

My father was a very gifted man. He was a veteran of "The War to End All Wars", successful in business and politics, and was well known for his grace and wit.

My mother was a beautiful Southern woman of her time. Contrary to the stereotype often seen in movies and on TV, she was not exactly a "hot-house flower".

As a young woman, she played golf well, hunted birds with the men, smoked cigarettes, and drank shots of whiskey like a cowboy. She was sent home from college for telling a tall tale in order to get to a dance that she wanted to go to.

During World War II, she ran her family's business while her brother was away in the Navy.

Later in life, she was an avid poker player.

In the years that it was my good fortune to grow up in her presence, she was a homemaker. Henry Ford didn't run his business any better than she ran that house. The house was spotless, the food was very good and was served on time.

During this period she was an archetypal Victorian lady, which makes it interesting for me to speculate on what she might have been like "before she was a virgin".

Mother had a list of "unsayable" words. These were words that must not be spoken. Aside from the usual list of curse words, there were others such as "belly", "nasty", and "pregnant" which were considered "tacky". "Nigger" was not on the list.

My older sister was a product of my father's first marriage. She was the only child of divorced parents in her school when she was growing up.

When my parents married, they "eloped" to New York City to be married by Dr. Norman Vincent Peale (a leading clergyman of that time) at the Marble Collegiate Church. This was, at least in part, to avoid the procedures followed by the Episcopal Church in that era for second marriages.

People who knew my father were not surprised by this extravagant gesture. Of course he would do it that way!

My family was in the textile business. We had a small knitting mill that employed something over a hundred people. It had been started by my grandfather in 1898, the year of my father's birth. Initially there had been other investors, but by the time I came along all of the stock was held by my father and his siblings.

One of the Mill's assets was a "modest" four bedroom "cottage" at Atlantic Beach, North Carolina. It had been built in 1946 at a time when the Internal Revenue Service could think of such things as business assets. I leaned to crawl at the cottage.

The twelve summer weeks that were defined as "the season" were divided equally among the four family members that represented the stockholders.

My first cousin Rob and I would go down to the cottage for a week or two with one set of parents then, when the time for a changeover came, we'd swap parents and stay for another week or two.

In the cottage's basement were the servants' quarters. My father and I would catch whiting, spot and flounder in the early morning surf in front of the cottage. Our catch would then disappear into the basement and reappear, fried, on the breakfast table along with eggs, roe, fried tomatoes, grits, toast and coffee.

We stood on the seawall and shot skeet that were thrown by my uncle with a hand thrower.

We ate from the sea and at night, if my father had a couple of extra drinks, we would sometimes swim in the ocean under the stars.

At this time in history there was not the profusion of mercury-vapor outdoor security lighting that there is today. When the sun went down it was dark. The stars and planets were spectacular and the Milky Way, which some urban dwellers never see today because there is too much light, was clearly visible. Surely there is a spiritual metaphor in this remembered experience.

Bobbing around in the ocean out past the breakers, we would sweep an arm through the water and marvel at the fiery arc caused by the phosphorus in the sea.

At the end of the row of cottages where our house was located was the Coral Bay Club. The Club had a pool, tennis courts, a boat dock, plenty of pretty girls, and a bar that would sell alcohol to one of my underage buddies. As teenagers we tried to get my father to join, but he refused saying that he was on vacation and wasn't going to any club that required him to wear shoes.

It had been a very wonderful and privileged life.

Rawls Howard
November 2017

Chapter 1

Mrs. Jenkins' 9ᵗʰ Grade English Class
December 1962

This weekend, you will write a three page paper on the story of your life. This work is due Monday morning.

I

    I was born on October 29, 1947 in Edgecombe General Hospital. I was the first son of Mrs. Madeline Jenkins Thomas and Mr. Adam Thomas.

    I don't remember the first few years of my life but the first thing that I do remember was when my grandfather gave me a key chain with a lot of old keys on it. I learned to crawl at our families' new beach cottage that was built the year I was born and I have been to the beach every year since. When I was two my grandfather died and I can remember missing him very much.

    I had a nurse since the day I was born and she was with me for what seemed 24 hours a day. She went to the beach with us every time and walked me up and down the beach.

She died when I was about five years old. That same year our family visited Washington, D.C. I don't really remember much about the trip except that we went on the riverboat, "The Old Bay Liner". While in Washington I remember visiting the Smithsonian Institute and seeing Lindbergh's plane and getting my head caught in the iron fence surrounding the White House. I still keep one or two souvenirs from that trip.

The next year our family took a trip to Charleston, South Carolina. I had been to Charleston before but this was the first trip I really remember. I can remember seeing the Cooper River Bridge for the first time and going to Fort Sumter.

The next year I was seven years old and right after my birthday I went shooting with Bip Carstarphen and shot a .22 rifle and a shotgun for the first time in my life.

Nothing very interesting happened to me then until I was ten years old.

II

When I was ten years old my parents took me to McAdensville to the Davidson College homecoming game. While there we visited with a family named Pharr; I guess these were just about the nicest rich people I have ever known. They lived in a house that had five living rooms, a kitchen, a dining room and

two bedrooms on the first floor. While I was
there I rode in my first sports car. We rode
very early in the morning and I remember
being very cold, especially since we were
going over 100 mph; that was the only time I
have ever been over 100. That made a big
change in my life. I will not take up sports
car racing as a profession but I'm thinking
of doing it as a hobby.

That next summer I went to Camp Morehead
for four weeks. I didn't like it very much
and even ran away from camp, but since I have
gone to a lot camps as I will tell later.

III

When I was twelve years old my chief
interest was hunting but I didn't have a gun
at the time. I actually don't remember going
hunting but twice that year and I went with
my uncle both times.

One other very important thing happened
that year. This was the year I started
confirmation classes. I finished the classes
and joined Thomas Memorial Presbyterian
Church.

At thirteen I got the Go-Kart bug and
decided that I just had to have one. Finally
on September 16, I got one. On the first day
I got it I'm afraid I treated it a little
roughly. I didn't wait for the motor to get
broken in, I just went ahead and drove it

almost as fast as it would go. Rob Thomas, who got his Go-Kart at the same time, is still running on his original motor. I drove the kart almost every day and soon learned how to drive fairly well. A group of Go-Kart owners got together often and had races. My Go-Kart has had seven bad wrecks so far with me driving and somehow I have come through them with just some torn clothes and bruises.

That year three things happened almost at the same time. First I got a new shotgun. I went hunting that same day and managed to shoot up four boxes of shells without hitting too much. Second I got a dog. I had a dog before but he died when I was very little. Anyway, this dog grew and kept growing until he was tremendous. Third I started taking saxophone lessons. I hadn't really thought much about music until one day the idea just hit me. The more I thought about it the better I liked it and I am still taking lessons.

I went to Camp Sea Gull that summer. The only person in my cabin that I knew was Rob Thomas but that didn't keep me from having a really good time. My counselor that year went to Davidson College and that impressed my father because he went to Davidson too.

I went to Camp Sea Gull this past summer too, but this year I was in the cabin with Jimmy Winslow and Tommy Thorne. We all had a good time. While I was at camp I met another cousin that I didn't know was down there. His name is Billy Transou. I didn't recognize him at first because I hadn't seen him in such a long time but in a little while we became friends and went sailing every day.

I didn't come directly home from camp; I went to the beach and shot firecrackers. The law really doesn't mind if you shoot firecrackers if the beach isn't too crowded, but the Fourth of July I got caught shooting firecrackers in Tarboro and people here do mind. The police didn't fine me since this was my first offense but they warned me.

I have had a very exciting life and think I wouldn't change a moment of it.

Chapter 2

The Outcast
November 1965

And Esau seeing that the daughters of Canaan
pleased not his father;
Then went Esau unto Ishmael, and took unto the
wives which he had Mahalath the daughter of Ishmael
Abraham's son, the sister of Nebajoth.[1]

I was startled awake by a very strange dream.

In this dream, I was walking under an overcast sky down a path that ran through rolling countryside. The landscape was bleak and there were no buildings or other people in this region.

Although I was on foot, I knew that I had access to my new wife's deceased father's car. The car was an unusual and fine two-door '62 Buick that had been custom made for him before his death.

It was white with a black vinyl top. The four speed transmission with floor mounted shift, a tachometer and the high performance engine made it a joy for an eighteen year old boy such as myself to drive.

---

[1] *Holy Bible*, Genesis 28:8-9 KJV

I knew that I would have to take this car to Raleigh in order to get my own car which was a red and white British sports car.

I also knew that my friend Eddie would go with me and help me, but that he should not be allowed to drive my car once we picked it up. He could handle the Buick at that point.

It was very important that I tell my father these things.

Then I woke up.

My father came to my bedroom door and said, "Son, I need to see you downstairs as soon as you can get dressed."

I nodded to him and saying nothing got out of bed and began to dress. I tried to remember what had happened the night before. The confusion of the dream and the echoes of my Mother's wails of anguish were tormenting my mind.

I had come in at 11:30 and found my father waiting up for me. He was smoking and playing solitaire in the sitting room.

Having fortified myself with a half-dozen bottles of beer, I had finally been able to tell him that Dinah was five months pregnant, and that I had married her in a civil ceremony in South Carolina the preceding weekend. As I had anticipated, the news was not well received. Not well at all.

"You were just looking for a license to sleep together," he had moaned. "I remember when I was your age that there were some girls that were for f-f-fucking, but you can't do this. Not to yourself, and not to us."

That had been the first time that I had ever heard any trace of the stammer that I knew that he'd had as a boy. "It's already done," I said quietly.

He looked at me with grim resolve. "You stay right where you are," he said. "I have to go and tell your mother."

He walked out of the room and I heard him start up the stairs. I lit a cigarette with my heart pounding in my chest and waited.

"Oh nooo!" came the wail. "Oh no! No! No!"

A few minutes passed and he returned. "We can't do anything about this tonight," he said sadly. "Go to bed and we'll talk in the morning."

I had climbed the stairs with my heart in my mouth, brushed my teeth and gone to bed without saying anything to Mother. I knew that she was in the next room and in agony, but I simply couldn't deal with her right then.

Now the sun was up on a new day and it was finally time to face the music.

Although I hadn't been aware of it, I had been moving toward this confrontation for the past several years. My seeming inability to give my parents what they wanted from me had resulted in an ever present friction between us. This tension had manifested itself in my bringing home an escalating string of problems. My father had dealt with these situations by buying my way out of them and sweeping them under the rug. It was as if they had never occurred.

In fact, Dinah was not even the first girl that I'd gotten pregnant. The one before her had simply been whisked away, disappearing from the face of the earth. At the time I had thought that there must have been an abortion. I had no way of knowing for sure since, as always, what had happened had not been discussed.

My father's old World War I army song, "Pack up your troubles in your old kit bag and smile, smile, smile," had once again been acted out in our home. This morning I was bringing him something that would not be fixed.

After I had finished dressing and brushing my teeth, I walked slowly down the familiar stairs. The living room on the other side of the hall was spotless as always, and the mahogany front hall table gleamed. The small silver plate with the car keys was centered next to the ever-fresh arrangement of cut flowers from the yard.

I turned into the living room with my heart in my mouth. My father stood in the middle of the room. Standing with him was Vinson Bridgers, a prominent lawyer in our community.

Mr. Bridgers was not my dad's regular lawyer who was a well-connected corporate guy.

No, Bridgers was another breed of cat. He was a courtroom scrapper, with a reputation as a very savvy litigator.

Herbert Taylor, Dad's regular counsel, had a national reputation in corporate law, but it was Bridgers who people called on when really unpleasant personal shit was in the fan.

This was the showdown.

Both men looked at me somberly.

I met my father's gaze.

He spoke first. "Son, you know that I love you. You have always been the apple of my eye. But there is something that you really need to know. This so-called marriage that you've entered into is something that your mother and I will not allow to happen. You and Dinah are both much too young and she is not the kind of girl that will ever be a part of our family. Mr. Bridgers has agreed to help us with this and we're going to get the marriage annulled. Do you understand what I mean by that?"

"I understand exactly what you mean," I replied. "I also understand that it's obvious to anyone looking at Dinah that it's much too late for that now. I will not agree to something that's so clearly wrong."

He looked at me. Then he looked down sadly. Then at Bridgers. Then back at me. He spoke slowly, "You are not going to listen to me on this. Legally there is nothing that I can do, but I need for you to understand something very clearly. If you do this, then you can no longer be a part of this family. You can no longer live here, and you and Dinah will *never* be Mr. and Mrs. Adam Thomas of 1101 Main Street. Are we clear on that?"

"Very clear," I replied.

"Go and pack your things then," he said grimly. "You will need to tell your mother goodbye."

I turned and left the room without saying anything. Back in my bedroom, I found an old suitcase with my mother's initials monogrammed on the leather binding.

Mercifully, I wasn't feeling much of anything at this point. I was numb.

After packing a few personal items, I marched slowly back down the stairs. They were waiting for me in the hall. My mother in tears. My father grimly determined.

"Adam, this is not what we want," my father said.

"I don't have any choice," I replied.

"This is crazy!" sobbed my mother.

"I'll need to come back in a few days and get the rest of my stuff."

"Call before you do that," Dad said. "You are not to come here without asking us first."

"Ok," I said. "Well, this is goodbye then." Turning, I started for the door, suitcase in hand. Behind me, I heard a sob, then the sound of running feet. My mother ran down the hall and jumped onto my back. Her weight carried us both to the floor in a heap.

I got back up and helped her up too.

"I'm sorry," I said, then I turned and walked through the door.

Walking down the front steps of the only home that I had ever known, I made a left turn and headed downtown. I wasn't thinking, but suddenly came to the realization that I had no idea what to do next. I was on the street with my clothes in my hand and nothing but a closed door behind me.

Not knowing what else to do, I did an about-face and walked back past the house toward Eddie's. He would have an idea.

Eddie was a couple of years older than me and had become someone that I looked up to after he had lost his driver's license for prearranged street racing in his father's car.

The race had been Eddie's idea. He and two other guys had used the front door of the Presbyterian Church fellowship hall for a starting line and had taken off through the center of town wide open with straight pipes roaring.

One car dropped out, but Eddie and his friend Bear raced through the business district coming within a block of the police station twice.

When they went by Len Robbins' house on their way out of town, Len saw them and called the cops.

On the outskirts of town they rounded a curve at over 100 mph and met a highway patrolman coming in the opposite direction.

They ran the patrolman off the road.

Eddie had stopped, but the police had to get Bear out of the movie theater an hour or so later.

This made them famous. They were just the kind of guys that appealed to me.

The air was crisp and clear on this November morning. I walked past the Victorian era homes that defined the part of town that was "mine". It had been mine for as long as I could remember, but would be mine no longer.

Leaving the residential section behind, I walked past God Damn Joe's Texaco station. My cousin Sam had christened the station with that name in appreciation of Joe's poetic inclinations for foul language. "When he wants to get snow-chains on a car," Sam had said, "He just puts them down next to the tires and cusses at them until they jump on."

I had never had to pay anything for gasoline, or anything else in Tarboro. I had just picked up whatever I wanted, said "charge it" and kept going. It didn't occur to me as I walked along that this would no longer be the case.

I didn't have a car anyway. The old MG had given up the ghost and Dad had balked at the '55 Chevy with the Corvette engine that I'd wanted to replace it with.

What was there to worry about? I had about $450 in cash in my pocket. I'd made that money playing saxophone with the Impaks and another couple of hundred in U.S. Savings Bonds in my lock-box. That was a small fortune in a world where the average man-on-the-street didn't bring home $100 for a week's work.

Actually, a week's work was something that I'd never done. Dad had gotten me a summer job at the Mill, but after the first day I'd refused to go back. He'd turned red as a beet and stomped out of the room.

No, the sax was my source of income. The band played little gigs around Eastern North Carolina and had steady work on weekends with the Moose Club and the American Legion.

I'd always had a pocket full of money. It's easy to accumulate money if you have an income and don't have any expenses. The only thing that I'd ever spent my own money on was entertainment. Beer and girls.

I walked along the street clueless. Within a month, my new wife would talk me into giving up my horn as something that was inappropriate for a married man.

One day, far in the future, I would realize that marital status has nothing to do with whether playing music is appropriate or not. The real problem was that she thought that the horn made me too attractive. It had, after all, been a part of what had made me attractive to her. But this was not that day.

I crossed over to the other side of the street and walked by the depot. A Seaboard Coastline engine was moving a tank car slowly onto a siding.

Passing Long Manufacturing and the "Ford Store", I saw Hiram Kelly on the used car lot. *Asshole.* The man was an asshole. We had blown up his mailbox because he was an asshole.

A year or so later a Federal cop rang my doorbell. I was alone in the house and had let him in. Standing in the sitting room, he had explained that he knew that I was involved in the crime. When he mentioned the possibility of reform school and asked who else was involved, I took a deep breath and named the rest of the guys in the car.

When he walked out of the front door headed across Main Street, I picked up the phone and dialed 3-2516 as fast as I could. Sam answered. I said, "Man you ain't gonna believe who's coming to see you!" For a few weeks after that, we were all famous.

Nothing came of it of course. That kind of trouble wasn't allowed in my father's house. Getting something like that in through the door was kind of like getting a snake into the Garden of Eden. It just wasn't going to happen. Now I'd finally gotten the snake in and my father threw it back out and me with it.

Anyhow, Hiram Kelly was an asshole. I didn't know why he was an asshole, but Eddie said he was, and that was good enough for me.

I rounded the corner and walked toward Eddie's. The Pattersons' was a light blue one story house on a corner lot. Eddie's rooms had at one time been a small apartment with a kitchen and separate entrance. Although it was directly connected with the rest of the house, this arrangement provided Eddie's place with a sense of palatial separation from parents. This contributed in a big way to the aura of larger-than-life uniqueness that surrounded him.

I walked to the end of the house and knocked on his door. It would take him awhile to answer. It always did. I'd never seen Eddie do anything in a hurry. I knocked again and he came.

Eddie was tall and lanky with curly black hair and peaceful brown eyes. He was well over six feet tall, taller than me in fact, and weighed only 160 pounds. It was easy to remember how much he weighed, because he had used a rigorous weightlifting routine to sculpt his body into a rock-hard piece of muscle. He had kept at this training until he could standing-press his own body weight. A remarkable achievement that was all the more remarkable because he had no interest in athletics, and was one of the most peaceful, non-violent men that I have ever known.

He almost never made a public display of his amazing strength and conditioning. The last demonstration that I could remember was his walking on his hands for about 50 feet down the leading edge of the roof of the two-story high school building.

"A.J.," he said smiling. "Come on in."

A.J. was a nickname that the boys gave me. It likened me to the race car driver A.J. Foyt. The guys were trying to stick me with it. I didn't like it and didn't encourage it, but I didn't argue about it either.

I came in and sat down.

Eddie looked at me. "What's wrong now?" he asked.

I explained the situation.

"You did *what?*" he exclaimed. "Man, you can't stay here! You can't even be here! Do you know what would happen to my parents if people thought that they were helping you with this?"

"I just need to call Dinah and get her to pick me up," I said.

"Well go ahead and do that now," he replied.

Forty-five minutes later she pulled up to the curb. I got behind the wheel of the white Buick and drove off into a new life.

Chapter 3

A Stranger in a Strange Land
December 1965

And Isaac his father answered and said unto him,
Behold, thy dwelling shall be the fatness of the earth,
and of the dew of heaven from above;
And by thy sword shalt thou live, and shall serve
thy brother; and it shall come to pass when thou shalt
have domination, that thou shalt break his yoke from
off thy neck.[2]

My wife and I were living with her younger brother and sister and her widowed mother. The house was a one-story brick home in a middle-class neighborhood.

Although I had been introduced to all of my new relatives in the course of picking Dinah up for dates, I soon found that living in the same house with this new family was much different than what I was used to.

The house was clean and neat enough, but gone was any trace of the heavy mahogany furniture, silver flatware and serving pieces, and the nicely arranged cut flowers that I had grown up with. Nobody appeared to be reading anything but the newspaper, and country music was usually in the air.

My very pretty young sister-in-law was astounded to learn that I had never heard of Hank Williams.

Rather than being at a set time, dinner was served at whatever time my mother-in-law got it ready. There were no servants, so the

---

[2] *Holy Bible, Genesis,* 27:39-40, KJV

serving dishes were put in the middle of the table and everyone helped himself. It was a little like being at summer camp.

No one in my new family could fathom my father's reaction to the marriage. I did my best to answer their questions without telling them straight out that my parents didn't think that any of them were on the same level as the Thomases. They were seen as members of a lower caste that could offer nothing to my parents except in the role of providing services of some kind to make them more comfortable. Not being stupid, my in-laws soon figured this out for themselves.

The irony of the situation didn't escape me. My parents were ashamed of me in my new situation, and I in turn was becoming ashamed of them. In time I would discover that these dark feelings would take all of us where we needed to go.

My wife and I had her old bedroom and her old double bed.

Whereas in my old life sex was something not to be mentioned, here it was happily joked about. This was somewhat disconcerting. I was used to having fun with "locker room" humor with the boys in the locker room, but not at the dinner table. I found that I could not get really comfortable with the new openness.

Dinah was seven months pregnant now, which added to my discomfort. I had the sexual impulses of an eighteen year-old boy, but didn't have any secure way of dealing with them.

It seemed to me that dinner conversation that wasn't about sex was about work. My in-laws were curious about what I might do to earn some money. They didn't spend time wondering what I might do to "fulfill my potential", but simply wanted to know when I was going to get a job. A job was simply that: a job.

I started going through the classified ads in the *Daily Reflector* circling jobs that didn't mention educational requirements. Surprisingly there were quite a few of these that seemed within reach.

A visit to the Grady-White Boat Company resulted in a job as a carpenter/boat builder on the assembly line that produced sport-fishing boats. I was to start work the following Monday.

I telephoned my parents and arranged to go by the house and pick up the rest of my belongings.

My wife and I made the trip together, stopping by the High School on the way to formally terminate my education.

Dinah waited in the car while I made repeated trips into my parents' house to get my things. The atmosphere in the house was heavy with unspeakable grief and disappointment. In the hour or so that this process took, fewer than fifty words were spoken.

The Buick was filled to overflowing with clothes, guns, saxophones, books, and other personal baggage from my old life.

There was nowhere near enough room in my new accommodations for all these possessions, but there was no way that I was going to put either myself or my parents though another home visit anytime soon.

At the end of my second work week at Grady-White, I lined up with the rest of the workers and was handed a pay envelope. This surprised me because, having heard people talk about a "paycheck", I had assumed it would be that.

Not at Grady-White. It was a small manila envelope with my name on the front. My gross pay, tax deductions and my net pay were all recorded in appropriate spaces in meticulously hand-written script.

Inside were bills and coins that had been counted to agree with the figures on the front of the envelope.

At the end the third week, both my employers and I were satisfied that I was definitely not a carpenter/boat builder and we agreed to part ways. This separation was perfectly amicable and I left with a good reference, which was the start of my discovery of the importance of maintaining a good reputation in the workplace.

I took this first good reference and, after a few more experiences of trial and error, found myself working as a route salesman for the Southern Bread Company. This job had the advantage of allowing me to work outdoors. It also involved driving a delivery truck, which I enjoyed. Another real bonus was that I spent my days driving around in a truck full of fresh bread, which smelled wonderful.

One Saturday in early February, my wife and I were in the living room talking when she began to have contractions. I bundled her and her suitcase into the Buick and we drove to the hospital, which was less than a mile away.

Her labor was long, but proceeded normally and by late evening we were a very happy family of three. She delivered a beautiful and healthy seven pound baby boy. We named my first son Christopher.

We had no health insurance of any kind, but the people at the hospital were very kind and seemed to take for granted that I would pay the bill in time. I was able to settle the debt before my son's second birthday, by making installment payments. Once this was accomplished, I could then joke about its taking so long that I'd been afraid that the hospital might've repossessed the boy.

During this process we found a wonderful old 1949 Plymouth automobile. The car was nearly as old as I was, but was incredibly well-maintained. It was gray in color, had a seemingly enormous interior, and of course a standard "three on the tree" gearshift mounted on the steering column. I found it irresistible and bought it at once.

As soon as I possibly could, I moved my new family out of my mother-in-law's house and into a small singlewide mobile home a few miles outside of the city.

This tiny residence had two bedrooms, an old window air conditioner, and a heating system that would run on kerosene. In cold weather, I would buy the kerosene five gallons at a time and carry it home in a military "jerry" can. We were very happy there.

On really cold mornings, the old Plymouth wouldn't start, but my landlord, a farmer named James Brown (like the singer) was always very kind and would help me get it going by jump-starting it with his pickup.

∞∞∞∞∞

My employer, knowing that I was from Tarboro and that I was well known there, gave me my hometown as part of my delivery route.

One day while in the process of stocking shelves at the A & P, I ran into my mother. When she saw me, her mouth dropped open, shocked at seeing me engaged at what she called "my menial job". We greeted each other briefly. Then both of us did an about-face and, being equally discomfited, got out of the situation as quickly as we could.

Mother had an eloquent way of talking and had a wonderful word to describe the work that my job entailed. It was "unseemly". Although I actually enjoyed the work that I was doing, I was very uncomfortable with her obvious shame at seeing me engaged in it. I asked my supervisor for another route just as one became available, and it was given to me.

This new route involved deliveries to schools and small country stores east of Greenville. I really enjoyed this work. I particularly liked working in the small country stores. I felt a natural affinity for the straightforward genuineness of the people that I found there.

One day a customer came into the store I was servicing and bought some dynamite, blasting caps, and fuse. Astounded, I waited until the customer left, then asked the proprietor how all of that worked. After all, fireworks were illegal at that time in North Carolina.

The store owner explained that it was perfectly legal to buy dynamite. All that was required was for me to give him the license plate number of my car.

He then proceeded to give me information on the different grades of the explosive (40% versus 60% nitroglycerine), the proper way to store it safely, and how to go about detonating it.

A short time later, I left the store with one stick of 60% nitro dynamite, one blasting cap, three feet of fuse, and a big smile on my face.

The following day was Saturday. I woke up early and headed to Tarboro. Arriving midmorning, I went straight to Eddie's. I knocked on the door and waited.

When Eddie finally opened the door, I was standing there with the stick of dynamite in my shirt pocket.

It took Eddie a second or two to realize what I had, but when he did he coughed once, then burst out in delighted laughter. "A.J., where in the world did you get that?"

I sat on his bed and told him the whole story, not bothering to point out the irony in the fact that dynamite was legal in a state where simple firecrackers were not. Eddie didn't need help getting that.

We made a quick phone call to Ty Hall. Ty was an important member of our cohort of guys who lived on the fringe of social normalcy. He was one of those people whom nature had endowed with tremendous physical strength. Standing about five-ten, he weighed two hundred and forty-five pounds. There was very little fat on his frame.

Ty did do some weightlifting, but it was not really a structured program. Lifting weights really served to validate his prowess, rather than to enhance it. He was the strongest man I ever met. He was born that way.

Eddie told him, "A.J. has come over and brought some dynamite."

"On my way," was all he said.

He had a real penchant for unflappable equanimity.

Forty minutes later, the three of us were wedged into Eddie's '58 MG headed for Bell's Bridge on the Tar River for our experiment.

Arriving at our testing ground, we prepared our charge with nervous exhilaration. There is something about being in a situation that has the potential for complete annihilation that brings on a sense of joy that is truly spiritual in nature. It would take many years for me to understand why this was, but that didn't keep me from enjoying it in that moment.

Being the only one there that had received instruction on the process, I proceeded.

I opened the dynamite's paper wrapper at one end. Then, using a pencil, I made a neat cavity in the sand-like explosive inside.

Next I inserted the fuse into the blasting cap and pressed the fuse and cap into the charge.

Finally, I tucked the paper wrapping around the fuse and made the whole arrangement secure with electrical tape.

Using a length of tobacco twine, we suspended the single stick of dynamite about six feet beneath a tree limb.

We had absolutely no idea how powerful one stick of dynamite was. What we wanted to find out at that point was how *loud* it was.

We lit the fuse and retreated with dignified haste to a distance of about two hundred yards.

After a period of several very long minutes, we were rewarded with a magnificent "boom!" There was noise, smoke, power and danger. Most of the things we knew and loved.

The three of us looked at each other in silent delight. There was giggling. Finally Ty spoke.

"More," he said, grinning from ear to ear.

"Let's get some beer and go somewhere and talk," said Eddie.

We got back into the MG and drove to Whitehurst Grocery to pick up some beer. We then sipped our way out to the old sandpit to do some target shooting.

The sandpit was a natural sand deposit that had been heavily mined by a construction company to get materials needed for commercial construction and road building projects.

What they'd left was a kind of manmade desert with some good-sized depressions that were fed by rains to make clear water ponds.

Some anonymous people had dumped a collection of derelict automobiles on the site. The rusting auto carcasses had gradually become a part of nature, blending into the landscape and creating the impression of an unspoiled wasteland.

We parked near one of the ponds and got out of the car.

Eddie had done a tour of duty with the Army in Vietnam, which had given him an advanced degree in firearms. He'd just gotten a new Browning Hi Power automatic pistol, which he had in the trunk of his car, along with a homemade mare's leg.

The mare's leg was an ordinary .22 rifle that Eddie had modified into a fully automatic weapon. He'd cut the barrel and the tubular magazine off at eighteen inches, cut and finished the rifle stock into a pistol grip, and filed the sear in the action to get it out of the way.

The magazine only held nine rounds now, but when you pulled the trigger the gun fired all of them in under two seconds. It was a lot of fun.

What was so remarkable however, was the fact that this peaceful man was so very skilled at coming up with this kind of toy.

Eddie laid both of the guns on the hood of the car and begin to teach.

"The 9 millimeter is the same diameter as the .38 Special," he explained, "but this round is a *lot* more powerful. Plus this thing holds fifteen rounds, where the old revolver only holds six." "And," he added, "you can have all the spare magazines you can carry."

Eddie opened a box of ammunition and began loading a magazine. Ty picked up another magazine and began loading that, and I did the same with a third.

Loading the three magazines pretty much emptied our only box of ammunition.

Eddie then racked a round into the chamber, threw an empty beer can as far as he could get it into the pond in front of us and began to methodically fire his pistol.

He used both hands to hold the pistol in what I would later learn was a Weaver stance. He sank the can in three shots, threw out a second can and sank that, then a third.

Ty took the next turn. He didn't do nearly as well as Eddie, but did manage to sink a can.

Then he handed me the pistol. This was the first time I had ever handled a center-fire pistol. I had fired .22 target pistols a couple of times, but had never fired anything this powerful.

I emptied the gun without hitting anything at all. It was pretty embarrassing. I had been a hunter all of my life, which was something that my friends were not, but I had never really learned to shoot a handgun.

"I've never had one of these," I lamely explained. "My folks wouldn't let me."

"Snake Man has one that he'd like to sell," said Eddie. "It's a Walther P38. A really cool gun. The Germans used it to replace the Lugar. You see them in a lot of spy movies. It's a 9 millimeter, same as this." He held up his own gun.

"How much does he want for it?" I asked.

"He told me he'd take ten dollars for it," Eddie replied. "There is something wrong with the slide, and he's too lazy to mess with getting it fixed. I don't know how much it'd cost to get it put right, but it's a hell of a deal."

Henry "Snake Man" Allred was a well-known local character. He was a few years older than me, a little older than Eddie too, and was definitely something out of the ordinary.

Like me, Henry had no interest in athletics. His main interests were classical music, literature, and science.

A salesman of medical supplies by profession, he devoted his free time to the study of the universe. Henry was passionate about astronomy, physics, and biology. He surrounded himself with telescopes, microscopes and culture dishes, and his home was full of literature on those subjects.

He was a naturalist. As a young boy he'd had a collection of turtles that he housed in an old iron lung in his parents' backyard. His nickname came from his love of snakes. He kept them as pets. At one time he had a full-grown python which he had been very fond of, and which had made a hell of a conversation piece. Particularly with certain types of girls.

Firearms and fast cars rounded out his interests.

Although Henry wasn't really a hunter, he kept a collection of guns. These were mainly for target shooting and for the study of the science of ballistics.

He was a neighbor of Eddie's, so, after finishing off the rest of the beer and firing a few full-automatic bursts with the .22, we drove over.

Finding Henry at home on weekends was usually not a problem. In a way, his disposition was a lot like one of his snakes. He could move very quickly and display a lot of energy when he was hungry, but between feedings he was wonderfully sedentary.

He answered our knock and affably produced the pistol. I did indeed recognize the weapon from its role in movies and was sold at once. The transaction took less than fifteen minutes, and we were on our way again. I already knew of a gunsmith in Greenville that could help with the repair.

The three of us parted company, after agreeing to make a run to the "dynamite store" that I'd found the following weekend.

∞∞∞∞∞

That week was a big one for me and my family.

I started a new job with Carolina Dairies as a route salesman, and we moved into a new house.

The milk delivery job was with the same company that my late father-in-law had worked for. He had been much loved there, and I'm sure that this family connection helped my job application a good bit.

The pay was much better than the bread business, and the nature of the work was different too.

Like the bread route, my customers were stores and supermarkets, but now I also serviced schools and made home deliveries.

I knew that the work was still "unseemly" from my parents' viewpoint, but I was making a better living and life was good.

The new house was a cinderblock, two-bedroom place about a mile closer to town than the trailer.

The rent, which was forty-five dollars a month, was actually a little less than what I'd been paying.

At first I didn't understand how I could be so fortunate, until I discovered that this home came complete with forty thousand cockroaches and water bugs.

I went to war with them at once, and as soon I was victorious, the little house became quite comfortable.

The new place was near the end of my milk route, and some days I'd stop by the house and let my wife and son ride with me for the last couple of school deliveries, dropping them off on my way back to the milk plant. This was very much against company policy, but it was fun, and we never got caught.

The boys picked me up the following Saturday morning in Eddie's car, and we headed out into the country to pick up some dynamite.

Eddie had taken the doors off of the MG and had found a World War I leather aviator's cap with the original goggles to complete his racecar driving ensemble. We were on top of the world.

That afternoon found us riding around Edgecombe County with a case of beer and a half case of dynamite, blowing up things.

After some smaller experiments, the Holy Spirit led us back to the old sandpit for a grand finale.

We found the carcass of an old 1953 Studebaker that was perfect for what we wanted. The tires, transmission, and engine had all been cannibalized for parts, and what remained was left in an open area with nothing that could be considered valuable anywhere near it.

Eddie duct-taped our remaining fifteen sticks of dynamite into a bundle. We then inserted the cap and fuse into the charge and made everything secure.

Reaching through the door of the old car, Eddie slid the package up the transmission tunnel, after first removing a small frog, getting it out of harm's way.

He then lit the fuse and we all retreated to a comfortable spot about two hundred yards away.

Opening cans of beer, we sat down and waited for the spectacle.

After several minutes, we got our reward.

The old car leapt off the ground, moving well before the sound of the explosion reached us.

The doors and hood flew off, and the top peeled back like a convertible.

The sound of the explosion was tremendous.

It was an experience of the sublime.

Chapter 4

Higher Education
June 1967

One Sunday afternoon my Uncle Winston stopped by the house. Winston was my mother's brother.

He was an elegant gentleman. A slim man in his mid-sixties, he would put on a fresh suit after lunch in the summertime in order to appear fresh, clean and dressed for business in the afternoon.

Winston would sometimes walk the few blocks down Main Street to his office in downtown Tarboro, but under no circumstances would he be seen carrying a package of any kind. That would spoil his deportment and create the impression that he might be engaged in physical work.

After saying good afternoon to Dinah and me, he inspected the baby, then sat down in our living room.

After a few minutes of settling in conversation, he explained why he had come. "Adam, I have an idea that I'd like for you to think about. Your father put aside some money while you were growing up that was to be used for your education.

"The money is in two irrevocable trust accounts at Edgecombe Bank.

"He's never going to accept your situation here, but the money is still sitting there. He couldn't touch it now, even if he wanted to.

"I think you should go to see him and tell him that you'd like to use it for the purpose he intended. I think he'll let you do that."

"Baxter Watkins is the Trust Officer at the Bank. He'll help you to manage what you have. It's not a lot, but I think it'll be enough for you to get through four years of college, provided you are careful and

Dinah is willing to get some kind of job to help you through this period.

"You need to finish your education son, and I'd like to help you with planning what you need to do, if you'd let me do that."

I thanked him for coming and told him that I'd think about the idea and call him the next day. He left us then, getting into his car and turning out of our driveway toward Greenville.

I sat back down to talk with Dinah, but I already knew what I was going to do before the conversation started.

I was happy with the life we had and the job that I was doing, but there was also something in me that knew that the rest of my life was too long to simply keep going along like I was. I had some unfinished business and I knew that I was going to have to take care of it.

The next day I called Winston. Then I made the call to my father. Dad and I arranged to meet at his office the following Saturday. We both wanted to meet in that setting to avoid upsetting my mother and to make it easier to keep our discussion on a business footing. As it turned out, it was to be the last time that I would see him there.

The meeting was brief.

He sat at his desk, which was a large mahogany antique that had belonged to his father before him.

This was his element. His place of power. Facing him in this place had always been much like facing a preacher in his pulpit.

He wasn't powerful on this day though. He had been defeated. The room was filled with his sadness.

We sat and looked at each other for what seemed like an eternity. The grandfather clock by the door ticked and the tropical fish swam in the aquarium by the window. Then he sighed and began.

He outlined a proposal just as Uncle Winston had suggested. It was really Winston's plan. It didn't him take long, but it took every ounce of his strength to get through it.

When I agreed to what was offered, we shook hands and I left. Both of us were spent. A new phase of my life was beginning.

The following weekend I met with the Bank's trust officer, Baxter Watkins. Baxter and I would be friends for many years.

Looking back, I realize that meeting with a bank vice president at his office on the weekend when the bank was closed didn't seem the least bit unusual to me. My father was on the bank's board of directors, and Uncle Winston was chairman of that board. The bank was in my hometown, and I'd always been a privileged person there.

I still am, though not in the same way.

∞∞∞∞∞

Life in Pitt County went on. Now, instead of delivering milk, I was selling building supplies in the daytime and going to the Community College at night preparing to take the state test for a high school equivalency diploma.

Dinah got a job at a local department store.

Bolstered by a stipend from the trust account, we moved into Greenville and rented a much nicer house that was around the corner from my mother-in-law.

Following Baxter's instructions, I went to the local Volkswagen dealer and bought a brand new VW "bug" - writing a check for the entire $2,000 purchase price. This car would provide reliable transportation for my college years without my having to worry about keeping an older car running.

I had taken the Walther pistol to a gunsmith who had repaired the original slide for a few dollars and also sold me a 6.5 millimeter Italian army rifle, proudly telling me that it was exactly the same kind of gun that had been used to kill President John Kennedy.

Then my father got sick. He got a sore throat down at the beach cottage that turned out to be cancer. He wasn't sick for very long. He took the radium treatments that the doctors recommended and he fought the disease, but when they told him that the disease had spread and would be fatal, he simply died.

My cousin Sam and Eugene Simmons, a close friend of our family, drove over to Greenville to tell me. When I saw the two of them walking up to my front door together, I knew why they'd come.

I let my wife know what had happened, got a few things together, and rode back to Tarboro with my friends. Gene was a tobacco warehouseman. He was also Sergeant-at-Arms in the North Carolina Legislature. He was much sought after as an "after dinner speaker" because of his wit and eloquence, and was the perfect man for the errand that he'd been sent on. I rode home to Tarboro in a cocoon of friendship.

The house was filled with people. Conversation was subdued. Servants moved through the crowd with trays of food and I could see that a second bar had been set up in the breakfast room.

I went to the sitting room and found my mother sitting in her usual chair, surrounded by friends. My father's chair was empty.

I kissed her, we hugged, and she told me that she was glad I was there. We then walked to the dining room.

My father's casket was at the other end of the room at the head of the table, and the room had been decorated with fresh greenery. My father's sister took me aside and said gently, "Honey, I want you to know that your father is not in that box."

Another aunt, Winston's wife, got hold of me and slipped me a pill that would numb my grief. "Our kind of people don't cry," she said quietly, but firmly.

I took the pill.

I had never been to a funeral in my life. This way of conducting one, with the casket at home, was from a different time. From a different era. It was from my father's time. It's part of a way of doing things that has now faded into the past.

Acting on Winston's instructions, my cousin Sam took me out the back door and drove me to W.S. Clark's Department Store. The store was closed but Sammy Harrell, the head of the Men's Department, was waiting for me. He outfitted me with a navy blue suit, several white shirts, a couple of red and blue striped ties, a few pairs of black socks, and a pair of black dress shoes.

Going back to the house, I went upstairs and rested for a while. An hour later, the suit had been altered and delivered. I got dressed.

Now I looked like I was supposed to.

Later that afternoon, my sister Meg and her family arrived from Charleston. My brother Ernest was with them.

Meg had spent most of her married life in Charleston, having married a truly wonderful guy from an old Charleston family and giving birth to three beautiful daughters there. Meg was twenty-one years older than me, and Ernest and I had grown up playing with her girls like siblings. I was mighty glad to see them all.

Ernest had been spending the summer with Meg. He was supposedly taking a summer course in algebra.

Actually, my brother, who was sixteen at this time, didn't need any extra help with algebra. He was *way* ahead of the curve with math. Meg had kindly agreed to the visit in order to give him some distance from the immediacy of his father's death.

We all gathered around Mother for an evening of remembrance of the amazing man who was my father.

The next morning, a short caravan of black vehicles arrived at our front door. My father's casket was loaded into the hearse by six of his friends and family members.

Ernest and I helped Mother into the car that followed immediately behind the hearse, with the rest of the family in the cars behind ours. The church was only six blocks away.

We parked and processed behind the casket into a standing-room-only crowd. The church gleamed with fresh paint, mahogany and polished brass.

There were no flowers in the sanctuary. Instead, the space had been filled with greenery. It was warm and beautiful.

I sat next to Ernest, who sat next to Mother, in the pew that had been my family's for five generations.

I really don't remember much about the service itself. Following orders, I didn't cry. I do remember, however, a huge tear leaving Ernest's bowed head and hitting the carpet. Thank God for that!

At the conclusion of the service, we followed the casket back out of the church to a thunderous rendition of Onward Christian Solders provided by the church's magnificent organ and a combined choir that came from all of the downtown churches.

The caravan then took us to a cemetery that was about two miles away where my father was interred with his parents, grandparents, and other members of our clan.

Everyone then went back to our home where things spooled up into a full-blown cocktail party.

The house was filled to overflowing and the crowd spilled out onto the porch. Elegant food was everywhere. Uniformed servants saw to everyone's needs.

The two bars were tended by the Ricks brothers.

Herbert Ricks had gone to work in my maternal grandfather's house when he was sixteen years old. He and his brother Ervin were identical twins. As alike as a pair of bookends.

When World War II broke out, Herbert brought his brother up to the house, showed him what to do, and went to serve his country. He was long gone before my grandmother knew about the switch.

Now Herbert worked at Uncle Winston's house.

The party lasted much longer than I wanted it to. Later on I had a quiet supper with my family, after which my cousin Sam gave me a ride back to Greenville. Back to my other family, and back into exile.

∞∞∞∞∞

The test for the equivalency diploma turned out to be no problem for me. With that piece of paper in hand, I resigned from my job at the building supply firm and became a full-time student. I would not work again for money for the next three years.

Winston advised me to study Liberal Arts (now called Humanities) for two years at a Community College, then transfer those credits to a four year school and get my terminal degree (now that's an interesting way of saying it!) in business.

I enrolled at the Lenoir Community College in nearby Kinston, piled all of our possessions in a U-Haul moving truck and set out with my wife and son.

We rented a nice little two-bedroom house and settled in easily. Dinah found a job at a nearby department store, and I began my coursework.

Since my funds were so limited, it was my plan to get the courses required for a four-year degree done in three years by working year-round taking a maximum course load. I figured that this plan should leave me with enough money left to buy gas to get home from school on.

My education was not to be the typical college experience. It was a means to an end. I was working for another piece of paper.

To my surprise, I found that I enjoyed my studies. The environment at the Community College was friendly and low key, and I began to make friends among both the students and the faculty.

Frank Cauthen was my French instructor. He had been a Commander in the Navy, and had learned most of his French in France.

He was also a member of Alcoholics Anonymous. He was very open about his alcoholism, telling stories to the class about his commanding a ship in the Pacific Ocean while drunk. Without getting a DUI. He also talked about his recovery from his condition.

When Mr. Cauthen found out I was from Tarboro, he asked if I knew Len Robbins. Len was a much loved member of my family who was also in AA. We formed a common bond based on this personal connection.

That bond served me well, since my aptitude for foreign languages is nil and it was all I could do to get through two years of the stuff. The really important things that I learned from Commander Cauthen had nothing to do with French.

Henry Bushwitz was a fellow student. A biology major, Henry had the appearance of a rather inquisitive bird. He was tall, thin, and bespectacled, with a shock of strawberry blond hair.

He had an affinity for animals and was a naturalist and a scientist. Somewhat like Henry the Snake Man from Tarboro. He was also a hunter. We had many adventures in the time that I lived in Kinston.

Another close friend that I soon made was Charles Bridgers. Charles lived around the corner from our little house. He wasn't a student. He was a fireman by trade, but what he really was was a hunter. Not just any kind of hunter though, Charles was a deer hunter. He had no interest in hunting anything else.

Charles' work schedule with the fire department was twenty-four hours at work, followed by twenty-four hours off work, and an extra day off a week. This was an ideal schedule for the life he wanted, and the job paid enough to support it.

Charles looked pretty much like a young, muscular Robert Mitchum (as he appeared in the movie *Thunder Road*). He had black hair that would hang over his forehead unless combed, and brown eyes. He moved with the ease and grace of a cat.

Charles had a pack of about twenty-five Walker deer hounds that he kept in pens in a disreputable part of town located on the property of a man named Lyman Grant.

Lyman Grant was the stuff of legend. He had reputed ties to gambling, prostitution and bootlegging. There were dark stories of men disappearing out the back door of his gambling house into the Neuse River, never to be seen again. He was a father figure for Charles. One of two.

Charles took very good care of his hounds. They were beautiful animals, some of which were "culls" from the pack of Percy Flowers, the famous North Carolina bootlegger.

The pack was fed on a mix of dry dog food, which was purchased in fifty pound bags, and slop that was gathered from the lunchrooms of several of the local public schools.

Twenty-five mouths are a lot to feed.

Much of the routine veterinary care that was needed was provided by Charles personally. Those animals were loved and cared for.

The bulk of Charles' hunting was done on some huge tracts of land, owned by the Weyerhaeuser Paper Company, near Aurora, North Carolina.

Charles hunted with the intensity of a revival preacher. When he found out that I was interested, and could help with some gas money, he started inviting me.

The firearms that I had at the time were useless for this kind of activity, so they were traded or sold. My new arsenal came to be a .30-30 lever action deer rifle, an over-under combination rifle/shotgun, and a single-action .22 revolver. I became proficient will all of them.

Actually, I became more than proficient with the revolver.

Whereas the ammunition for the Walther pistol had been too expensive to allow for much practice, .22 shells were a dollar a box.

I practiced a lot, and there were a lot of night expeditions with my friend Henry to collect frog legs. Henry had little or no money and he would sell the frog legs to restaurants for two dollars a pair.

Henry and I had many of this kind of "Mark Twainish" adventures together and became as close as Tom & Huck.

Of course these nighttime outings were not strictly for profit. We'd take along enough beer to keep our spirits up and would also make time for shooting feral cats (feral cats being the enemies of the local quail population) and for "Yellow-hammerin'".

Yellow-hammerin' is an old Southern sport, where the participants climb into the rafters of tobacco barns at night. Then someone picks up a sleeping bird from a rafter and the players play catch with the animal. If you pick up the wrong bird however, an owl for example, you'll really wish you hadn't.

Along the way, Henry and I made contact with the local authorities, who asked for our help with eliminating a pack of savage dogs that lived in the Lenoir County version of the old sandpit that I knew at home.

These dogs were second and third generation wild and were genuinely dangerous. The "call of the wild" had taken over.

This local sandpit was much closer to town than the one in Tarboro, actually bordering the town. There had been incidents of the pack coming into the neighborhood that adjoined the pit.

The two of us went to work at once, making it a part of our routine to make a pass through the area on a regular basis.

On one of these trips, we stepped out of Henry's truck to get a better look at some movement in the distance.

Identifying the movement as three wild dogs, I reached back into the truck for my revolver, which was in its holster on the seat.

Grabbing the holster, I pulled the gun toward me.

Sliding out of the holster, the revolver fell to the floor of the truck. Landing on its hammer, it went off.

I felt something hit my hand and the bullet passed through the roof of the truck.

Looking down, I saw that my hand was a bloody mess and almost fainted. We wrapped a cloth around it and got to the local hospital as fast as the old truck would take us.

Because my hand was in a curved position to grab for the gun, the bullet had passed through my hand twice. Once through the skin at base of two of my fingers and again through the fleshy part of the hand behind my thumb.

Miraculously, all I had was what the movies call a "flesh wound".

I use the word "miraculously" in all seriousness, since I had managed to put all these holes in my good right hand without hitting any of the multitude of bones that would have left me crippled.

The hospital bandaged my hand and put my arm in a sling and I got to walk around like a wounded soldier for about a week.

In January of that year, we went up to Seven Springs, North Carolina. There we stole a flat-bottomed wooden Johnboat for an overnight duck hunting trip down the Neuse River.

The weather was very cold and we drift-hunted the first day, then spent the night on a sandbar.

We tipped the boat on its side with the end of a sheet of heavy-duty plastic under it, braced it, and stretched the plastic sheeting to make a lean-to to sleep under.

The next morning the weight of the snow had pulled the plastic down until it was resting on our legs.

It was the coldest I can ever remember being.

I don't remember how many ducks we killed on that trip, but by the time we got back to Kinston the next day I was cured of the duck hunting bug.

Not long after that Henry's best friend, a guy named Bud, separated from his wife. Henry, being the supportive friend that he was, let Bud move into his house temporarily.

But Bud not only moved into Henry's house, he moved into his bed as well and Henry's marriage broke up too.

Henry was so emotionally destroyed that he was unable to function. He dropped out of school and became unreachable to me and his other friends. In the end, he literally ran away and joined the circus (which was passing through town) and I never saw him again.

∞∞∞∞∞∞

With Henry now gone from my life, I began to spend more time with Charles.

The hunting trips to Aurora picked up and it was wonderful spending time in this untamed area. There were plenty of deer. There were tracks from bear too. I never ran across a bear, but saw foxes from time to time, and once saw two bobcats.

The experience of hunting with a pack of hounds is one that I shall never forget. Charles would spot fresh deer tracks on one of the logging roads that crisscrossed Weyerhaeuser's huge estate and "put in" there.

He'd walk his lead hound into the woods at that point. The rest of the pack would follow these two comrades. The lead dog, understanding what was expected of him would "open" on the scent with a full-throated cry. At once, other members of the pack would join in and the chase was on!

Charles and the rest of the hunters would then try to anticipate the course that the chase would take and to "cut off" the deer and get a clear shot. Charles, the huntsman, would recognize and call out the cries of the individual dogs in his pack.

I would join in the process, but in all of the many hunting trips that I made with Charles and his hounds I never killed a deer. That was not actually why I was there.

There is something about the "music" made by a pack of hunting dogs that unites with an animal part of me. I would listen and become one with them. It is thrilling. Truly spiritual in nature. It cannot be explained.

∞∞∞∞∞∞

My school work progressed on schedule and I made an application to the University of North Carolina at Wilmington to complete my college studies. The application was accepted and my wife and I began making plans to move.

It was during this time that I made the acquaintance of my friend Charles' other father figure.

Alexander (the only name I was ever told), was an older man, well into his sixties. He was tall, thin and hard as a rail, with gray hair and gray eyes that matched his hair. He had the eyes of a wolf. Charles always called him simply "Old Man".

Charles told me many times that the Old Man could get through the woods with such ease and speed that, despite the age difference, he couldn't keep up with him for very long.

I never witnessed this personally though. The only time I was ever in the company of the Old Man was on nighttime game poaching trips. These trips had nothing to do with sport. It was meat hunting pure and simple.

The three of us would take Charles' truck out into the county where we'd locate deer standing in fields feeding.

The Old Man would put a spotlight on one of them. The animal would stand there, literally like "a deer in headlights", and Charles would do the shooting.

Then we'd throw the animal in the back of the truck, take it to the dog pens and dress it. The meat went to the Old Man.

As I was nearing the end of my time in Kinston, we were out on one of these poaching trips, when a pair of headlights appeared behind us as we were leaving the scene of the crime.

Charles saw them first, then the Old Man, then me. No one said anything, but Charles' foot found the floorboard. He didn't go more than a mile before he made a hard left turn across an unpaved driveway and roared out onto an open field.

The headlights made the turn onto the field too, but then stopped, apparently unable to pursue across the field. Whoever it was must have been driving a sedan.

Charles drove full-throttle straight for the back of the field. When he was almost there, he slowed down and picked out a path through the woods. He knew *exactly* where he was and exactly where he was going.

That path led to another one and we soon found ourselves on a paved road, headed home.

I had outrun the cops twice before in my life, but never this way.

Charles drove straight to his house. We were no longer running full tilt, but there was no wasted motion either. I don't think anyone had said anything.

As the deer was put onto a piece of plastic sheeting, Charles' wife and daughter appeared.

Charles spoke a few words to his wife that I couldn't make out, and she melted away taking the little girl with her.

We carried the deer inside to a small bathroom and put it in the bathtub.

Then Charles and the Old Man pulled out their knives and went to work.

I had been around the field dressing process many times by now, but wasn't prepared for this experience. The stench of the innards and the sheer volume of the blood and guts in that very small room was incredible.

The sight of those two men, stripped to the waist and up to their armpits in gore was unforgettable. I was glad that the tiny bathroom was too small to accommodate all three of us.

I stood outside the bathroom door and ferried buckets of blood and guts to the backyard where I dumped them into a fifty-five gallon drum.

What I got that night was a close quarters initiation into an aspect of nature that most people in this age of boneless-skinless chickens never see. It was primal.

Most people, including "nature lovers", think that there is "nature", and then there is "human nature", and that these are two separate things. I know for a fact that they are not. We are a species. We are omnivorous, and we are predators. I not only saw all of that that night, but felt it as well.

There was something powerful in play that night. Much more powerful than a simple butchering job. The look on Charles' face as he worked on that carcass in that bathroom was exactly the same look that he had when he saw the headlights behind us on the road.

I never saw the Old Man again after that night. I would see Charles from time to time for a year or so after we moved to Wilmington, but I would never doubt for one minute what he might be capable of. After all, he'd already been to prison (some years before) for shooting one cop.

∞∞∞∞∞∞

Living in Wilmington was a wonderful experience for me. A small Southern city, it was nevertheless a much bigger place than I had ever in lived before.

Located on the North Carolina coast where the Cape Fear River meets the Atlantic Ocean, there are both beaches and a historic downtown area to enjoy.

I had visited there as a small boy, but seeing the city through the eyes of an adult was exciting. The place was alive with art and commerce.

We rented a two-bedroom apartment in a new complex near the University. Apartment living was new and different and exciting too! There was a swimming pool and clubhouse and we quickly made new friends there.

Dinah had no trouble getting another department store job about a mile from home, and Chris was placed in a daycare center where some of the other children from the apartments were also enrolled.

Following Uncle Winston's prompting, we called on people that were part of my family's connections in the city. There were drinks and polite conversation out at Orton Plantation and in several of the fine old downtown homes.

More fun was to be had with our own circle of new friends though. There were parties, oyster roasts, and trips to Wrightsville Beach.

My classes at the University were much less inspiring however. At Winston's direction, I was now focused on the study of business. I never really enjoyed any of these classes, as I've never really been very interested in business. I found myself grimly plowing through them with my eye on the finish line.

Cay Haun, a fellow student and fellow resident of the apartment complex, came to my rescue. We became friends and he provided me with opportunities to pursue and expand my interests in firearms, ballistics, and hunting.

Cay was a native of east Tennessee, who had joined the Coast Guard in his hometown. His idea had been to avoid going to Vietnam by getting a job in the military guarding the TVA dams near home.

Once in the service though, he'd been overcome with a totally unexpected fit of patriotism and volunteered for a tour. He had ended up jumping onto junks with a pump shotgun in the Mekong Delta.

After his discharge from the Coast Guard he settled in Wilmington, having been stationed there.

I've always been a passionate Southerner and a lover of Southern accents. Cay's was a beaut. He was a son of east Tennessee, and twanged like a banjo.

The two of us developed a foundry for the manufacture of center-fire ammunition for rifles, pistols and shotguns.

There were machine presses for reshaping and reloading fired brass rifle and pistol cases. Other presses would perform the same function for spent shotgun shells.

There was a small furnace for melting lead automobile wheel weights, which we bought in fifty pound lots. The melted lead alloy was then cast into bullets for rifles and pistols.

There was an inventory of different types of gunpowder, usually totaling ten to fifteen pounds. Primers were bought by the thousand.

My modest arsenal was expanded to include rifles, pistols and revolvers from .22 to .45 caliber. I also acquired shotguns for both hunting and skeet shooting.

Both Cay and I were member of the local gun club.

I read and studied the science of ballistics endlessly, spending much more time with this pursuit than I did with the dull business studies at the University.

Looking back now, I realize that I was fully under the sway of the Roman god Vulcan. Vulcan is the god of fire and destruction, who lives in a volcano. He is a blacksmith, who works with fire and metal. He is the armorer of the gods.

At the time though, all I knew was that I was obsessed with shooting. Particularly long-distance shooting with rifles and pistols.

The hunting was there too of course, including the needless killing of animals for fun. I have heard that the cat is the only animal besides humans that behaves this way. I don't know if that's true, but I'm sorry to say that this practice continued for about another decade before environmental awareness did away with it.

Thoreau wrote about the sport of hunting, which he said had been a rite of passage in his life. Something that he did at a particular time. He said that he had no problem with hunting but simply didn't do it anymore.

My position is exactly the same as his. I do miss the taste of wild game though.

∞∞∞∞∞∞

In due time my study of business came to an end. I got an interview for a job with the retail finance division of a large national corporation. On the evening of the interview, I put on the navy blue suit that Winston had bought for me for Dad's funeral (there is real irony there!) and met the company representative for dinner at an elegant downtown restaurant.

He offered me a job with a starting salary that was well above the average and I was off into the world of business.

Chapter 5

The Company Man
September 1971

I was now an employee of the General Electric Credit Corporation. What made this job different from the jobs that I had held before was it required "credentials" in order to get it. Even though I was a Field Representative, and would spend most of my time working outside with customers and appliance dealers, I was also "office help".

Essentially I was a bill collector, but I was one who also kept tabs on appliance dealers who financed their inventories with the company.

The company, GECC, moved me and my family to Greensboro, North Carolina, where we rented another apartment and I began my training.

My boss, Andy Anderson, and the other people that I was working with were all upstanding, honorable people, which made the transition to this new phase of my life as easy and pleasant as possible.

Learning to talk with people who were past due with their payments was an awkward experience at first, but Andy was a good and patient teacher, and I soon became comfortable with my duties.

The other Field Representative at this office was a man named Joe Fryberg. He was a Jewish man of about my age who was also a part-time college student. Joe was senior to me by virtue of his experience with the firm, but he, like Andy, was kind and patient with me.

Being from Tarboro, which had a very small Jewish population, I had never had much direct exposure to the Jewish culture. I found it delightful.

Joe's antics at the office Christmas party remain pleasant memories for me, and my interactions with his father were priceless.

Old Mr. Fryberg was an archetypal little Jewish man who ran a kosher grocery store in the city.

Joe and I would stop in there to borrow his van on occasions when it became necessary for us to repossess merchandise from a delinquent account (which was infrequent at this GECC office).

On one of these visits, we found Mr. Fryberg in conversation with a family friend.

"Hiram," said the friend, "that radio up there looks exactly like the one that we gave Joey for his bar mitzvah."

"That's because it *is* the radio that you gave Joey for his bar mitzvah," old Fryberg replied.

Joe was nonplused, but after the friend left, he said, "Father! You shouldn't have told Mr. Hurwitz that we're selling the bar mitzvah presents!"

"What?" replied his astonished father. "We're turning them into money!"

Joe and I had a wonderful time recounting this episode to the people back at the office after we had completed our mission with the van. Joe was a great guy who was completely comfortable with his heritage and taught this goy that the best Jewish jokes are told by Jews.

After only three months in the Greensboro office, Andy and a senior company man sat down with me.

There were problems in the Fayetteville office and I was offered a promotion and a very significant raise if I would agree to move there.

I agreed at once.

∞∞∞∞∞

The next day I drove down to Fayetteville to meet my new boss.

Allen Waters was a handsome man. He had olive skin, black hair and brown eyes. Anyone looking at him could tell at once that he had some Native American blood in his line.

His suit was somewhat flashy and he wore gold jewelry. A watch, rings, and a gold chain around his neck.

He got me settled in a motel across the street from the office where I had a chance to relax a bit before dinner.

He picked me up in his new Buick Riviera (a flashy car to go with the rest of him), and we went to a nice restaurant out on Bragg Boulevard for drinks and a lobster dinner.

We got along just fine, and after dinner he took me to a topless bar for more drinks and some local entertainment.

Fayetteville, North Carolina in the 1970s was an amazing place. Much, if not most, of the local economy was geared to helping the enlisted service men stationed at nearby Fort Bragg with establishing and maintaining as debauched and hedonistic a lifestyle as they could possibly manage.

Riding down Bragg Boulevard, one would see a pawn shop, next to a massage parlor, followed by a topless bar, then a motel (many with hourly rates). This general business pattern extended for a distance of several miles.

Allen told me that I'd arrived only two weeks after the authorities had closed the topless shoeshine parlor. I'd missed it.

Hay Street in the downtown district was the same business model on steroids.

Prostitutes walked the streets nightly, and on military payday they would invade the district in swarms.

If you stopped at a traffic light, a green-haired black girl might jump on the hood of your car to ask if you wanted a date. She could manage do this while emphatically assuring you that, "I ain't soliciting!"

In the eleven months that I lived and worked in Fayetteville, I was the only male in that GECC office that didn't have the clap.

After many too many drinks, Allen dropped me back at the motel and I wobbled up to my room and passed out.

The next morning I called the office to tell Allen that I'd enjoyed myself and was looking forward to working with him.

I learned that he'd driven the Riviera into a telephone pole on his way home after dropping me off and had knocked most of his teeth out on the steering wheel. He was at the dentist's office.

I drove back to Greensboro.

∞∞∞∞∞∞

After moving to Fayetteville, my home life underwent some significant changes.

We found a really nice house a few miles out of town, with a small lake in the backyard. It was by far the nicest place that we'd ever had.

I now had a company car to drive, which made us a two-car family. My son Chris enrolled in the first grade at a public school that was only two blocks from the house, and my income was enough to make it unnecessary for my wife to work outside of the home.

Not having any friends, other than the people at the office, my shooting and hunting activities were sharply curtailed. My friend Cay was living in Raeford, which was some distance away, so we didn't see each other very often.

I did make a couple of trips to Raeford to do some dove hunting with him. He was running with a crowd that would bait fields with trashcan lids full of cracked corn to attract the birds. These baits would be taken up a few days before the shoot so that the shooters wouldn't be arrested. The hunting was excellent. One day Cay and I shot five limits of birds between the two of us. There weren't many of these trips though, and the two of us gradually drifted apart.

Without any conscious intention on my part, I redirected the energy that I'd been spending on hunting and shooting into my job.

The Fayetteville office was a mess. A crooked furniture and appliance dealer had managed to stick the General Electric Company with over four million dollars in bad contracts.

With the help of a drunken, and probably complicit, credit manager at GE, he'd gotten approvals on contracts that had no chance whatsoever of being collected. In some cases he'd written up bottled LP gas as living room furniture and his friend at GE approved the contract. The customers on these contracts were very poor people. Most of them were black. It was a real disaster.

Several days a week I would rent a U-Haul truck, and my helper and I would work from morning until night repossessing truckloads of furniture and taking them to the company warehouse.

It was grueling and frustrating work, but I turned out to be good at it. The man who had my job before me had been fired because he couldn't take it and had finally snapped.

He'd repossessed some living room furniture from a poor family and piled it up in the middle of the street in front of their house. He'd then chopped it up with an axe and set it on fire. I could understand his frustration.

Not all of the work was this disheartening though. Most of the accounts that I dealt with were simply honest people, a lot of them in the military, who had overextended themselves. Most of them had committed every last nickel of a two-income budget, then one of the couple had lost his job. A pregnancy might do that. I could usually help people to work their way out of a mess like that.

Then there were the rural accounts. These were contracts that had been made by small town stores with country people, most of whom they knew. Just as I had found when working the rural areas around Greenville, I liked these folks. A lot of them were Lumbee Indians.

The Fayetteville office's service area included a big part of North Carolina's Sandhills region. Lumberton, and the small towns just west of there. There were beautiful places like Fair Bluff, North Carolina. I liked being there. These places more than offset time I spent in the rough neighborhoods in Fayetteville. Neighborhoods that I had to leave before sundown in the interest of safety.

My work got good results, and in less than a year I was approached by another senior company man about yet another move. This time it was to be Columbia, South Carolina, where another office was in trouble.

I was told that although the company needed for me to move immediately, they wouldn't be able to give me another salary increase right away. Instead they offered another financial incentive.

At that time, General Electric paid its field representatives a salary plus something called "Chinese overtime". Hours worked beyond the regular forty hour week were compensated, but at a *decreasing* rate.

For work done from forty to fifty hours we were paid half-time. For the hours from fifty to sixty, the rate was quarter-time, and so on. I'm still not sure how this was legal, but what the company offered me as an incentive to move was the time-and-a-half overtime rate that the rest of the world was getting. I knew that I'd be working a lot of overtime, so I agreed to this proposal.

As it turns out, the reason that I couldn't be given a salary increase was that I was already being paid at the top of my pay grade. This "special" overtime arrangement was to prove to be my undoing.

The Columbia office Branch Manager, a man named Bob Bracken, had me rammed down his throat.

Once I was there, the job had me working all the overtime that I could physically do in order to bring some order to the chaos of all the delinquent accounts. From the beginning, my paycheck was bigger than my boss'.

I did a lot of field work alone and at night. I hadn't been there long before I injured my back while trying to repossess a large window air conditioner by myself. This was an injury that would plague me for the rest of my life.

I went to a local doctor who told me that I had ruptured a disc, and ordered me to go home and lie down for six weeks. I couldn't believe that it would take that long to heal, but it did.

During this period of convalescence, we discovered that my wife was pregnant. We had a second child on the way. This was happy news, but our joy was severely hampered by our worries about my work situation and my health.

Before I had fully recuperated from my injury the Branch Manager came to my home and fired me.

My wife and I decided that we'd had more than enough of Columbia, and decided to move back to Wilmington. There was no job waiting for me there, but we both liked the city. It was the closest thing to home that I'd known since leaving Tarboro.

We left Columbia with my pregnant wife driving our Oldsmobile station wagon and my son Chris in the front seat beside her. I was laid out full length in the rear of the car.

Chapter 6

Barbara
April 1973

Vocatus atque non vocatus, Deus aderit[3]

In looking at my life in retrospect, I'm amazed at the omnipresence of God in the course of events that eventually led me to where I am today. For most of the time, I was completely unaware of Its presence, which affirms my present position with regard to the nature of God as the non-dualistic ground of Being that continually acts in and through all things. In the words of the *Upanishads*, It acts, "…in every movement of mind or body." It does this without requiring things such as belief, faith or worship. This positon is certainly much different from the teachings of my conventional Calvinist upbringing.

The absolute joy that I get from my spiritual life today, comes in the form of a rapturous amazement at the perfection of the way that things are (and have always been).

My wonderful father-in-law, who is at this time in his life a conventional Christian, told me of his experience at Self-Realization Fellowship[4] at an earlier point in his journey. He said that, "The most common response to enlightenment was to burst out laughing." I can understand that reaction. Reality really is very funny.

---

[3] Desiderius Erasmus, "Bidden or unbidden, God is present."
[4] Self-Realization Fellowship is based on the teachings of Paramahansa Yogananda, a Hindu saint.

As we rolled into Wilmington, there didn't seem to be much to laugh about though. I had very little money, no job, and no place to call home.

I was very scared, but was trying to put up a manly front for my wife and son.

Some friends in Wilmington gave us shelter in their home while we found our feet.

I found a miserable little job selling automobile tires to get some money coming in while applying for other work. I see clearly now that even this unhappy job was an indispensable part of the process that took me into a different phase of my life. Like everything else, it was perfect.

Dinah and I then experienced a series of amazing "coincidental" happenings.

First, we went to look at a rental house that was located on the fringe of a country club neighborhood. We met the owner, a woman who now lived across the street from the property that we were interested in. She looked us over, and then told us that she wanted us to have the house.

She then said that we could move in and that, instead of renting the house to us, she would prepare an agreement and the monies that we paid her would go toward our ownership of the property. She stated simply that this was the way that she'd gotten the property in the first place, and that she very much wanted to pass her good fortune on to us.

Next, I responded to a classified ad for a job and was hired as an Accounting Supervisor at the District Office of a national firm that was engaged in the sale of fertilizer and farm chemicals. The sales area was large, covering operations in both the Carolinas, plus small parts of Virginia and Georgia.

The nature of the business, and the nature of my duties there would turn out to have profound significance in the chaotic course that my life would take in succeeding decades.

Then, out of the blue, I got a telephone call from my mother. She said, quite simply, that she was tired of the separation and would like to meet my wife and son and establish a normal relationship with my family.

This hundred and eighty degree change in position was completely unexpected. After I was able to recover at least some part of my composure, I told her that I would like to have her as a part of our life as well.

We talked for a few minutes, but I was frankly too off-center to fully accommodate this new reality in our lives. I did manage to tell my mother that things were going well in Wilmington, and that we were expecting another child.

I could hear the pleasure in my mother's voice at this news, and we ended the conversation by arranging for a family visit to Tarboro the following weekend. My exile was over.

∞∞∞∞∞

Pulling my car up at the curb next to my family's home in Tarboro was an emotional experience for everyone. For me it was like returning to the womb.

My son Chris' mouth dropped open in amazement at the size of the house, and my wife laughed out loud at his reaction.

The house is not particularly large, nor does it have any historical significance, but it was over twice as big as anything that Chris had ever lived in. His child's eyes saw a castle.

Mother met us on the porch, and we all went inside.

I don't think I'd been back there since my father's funeral.

It was as if nothing had moved. The same mahogany, silver, and brass appointments. The same fresh-cut flowers from the yard. The same muted sense of security and well-being.

No servants were in evidence however.

We walked through the hall to the little sitting room. At Mother's prompting, I went to the bar and fixed drinks for the adults and we sat down.

Drinks and conversation had always been integral parts of my family's daily life. The cocktail hour was as regular as the sunrise and as natural as brushing your teeth. I don't have any unpleasant memories of this ritual. Over-indulgence was rare, and when it did happen I might simply notice that my father was standing with one foot resting over his head on the mantelpiece and balancing a piece of burning newspaper on his nose.

We talked. The conversation was awkward for a bit, but the alcohol calmed the waves and things got better. Mother and I carried most of the weight of making this strange situation as comfortable as possible. Chris helped quite a bit with the acclimation too. When the conversation wandered around to Mother's weekly ("penny ante") poker game with her friends, Chris wanted to know if that was how she made her money. This delighted his grandmother no end.

After a drink, we got our luggage from the car and I took my family upstairs.

I settled Dinah and me in the guestroom. Chris would have my old bedroom and my old bed. This had a kind of "otherworldly" feeling for me that was extremely pleasant.

When the clock said 6:30, everyone started moving downstairs. 6:30 was suppertime, and all of Mother's trains ran on time.

Mother had laid out a nice supper of chicken salad in the breakfast room. The silver was still silver, the china was still china, the crystal was still crystal, and the linen was still linen, but she hadn't insisted on using the dining room.

We'd always had good food when I was growing up. Mother was a good cook, and she had always had a black cook to help her for two meals a day (which two meals changed with the seasons). With the death of my father, Mother's financial circumstances had changed radically, but the food was still good and she never complained.

After supper, I took Chris out in the backyard and showed him the bunkhouse. The bunkhouse was an addition to the house that my parents made in the 1950s. They extended the detached outbuildings on the property with a seventy-five foot room that was originally intended to house an enormous electric train set that I'd been given by one of my aunts. The addition had its own bathroom. The house's heating system had been expanded to include the new space, and when we got air conditioning, the bunkhouse was included too.

The train set didn't work out very well, as it required too much mechanical expertise, which was not one of my father's gifts.

Two bunkbeds were then constructed by the Mill's carpenter, and the room was converted to a place for overnight "sleep-ins" for Ernest and me. It became a wonderful repository for any kind of "gear" that growing boys might need.

There were BB guns in their racks on the wall. There was all kinds of camping gear: tents, camp-stoves, hatchets, knives, and sleeping bags. There were dog collars, leashes and whistles. There were models of guns, planes and ships that Ernest and I had made as boys. There was a TV and a stereo system. And finally, there was a great feeling of home that brought tears to my eyes.

Chris had no trouble making himself at home there.

Then, Dinah and I helped ourselves to a beer and did the dishes. Drinking after supper was generally discouraged by my parents, except at the beach. However, drinking beer was not considered really drinking. It was a kind of soft drink. Anyway, it was definitely a special occasion.

Mother came to the kitchen and talked while we worked. She said, "There is a group of boys who live down on Saint Patrick Street (two blocks from our house) that are Chris' age. They play together all the time, all over town. They are all good boys and have a lot of fun. I called Betty Little, and she told me to bring Chris down in the morning, and she'll introduce him to her son John and get him started."

Betty Little was the wife of Mayo Little, who was the Rector of the Episcopal Church that Mother attended.

At that time in history, Episcopal ministers were not referred to as priests. At least not in Eastern North Carolina. A priest was something that a Catholic would have, so no Episcopalian was going to have a priest. Not in this lifetime.

The next morning after breakfast, Mother did as she promised. We didn't see Chris again until suppertime. Chris is now over fifty years old and is still friends with those guys.

Dinah and I spent the morning walking around town. Small town Southern life can be surprising to people who aren't used to it. It's warm, welcoming and friendly. People will not only speak to you on the street, they'll stop and talk to you too. My wife and I ran into half a dozen people that I knew and the time passed quickly and pleasantly.

We were careful to be home a little before noon however, because we were expecting a visit from Uncle Winston and his wife Virginia.

Noon on Saturday was drinking time again for my family. Drinking during the day on weekdays was not sanctioned, but the weekend was different. In fact, there was a horn that sounded from the top of the Town Hall to remind you when to start.

Winston always said that, "Anyone who has more than one drink in the daytime is crazy," and would always stop with one. I don't think I ever did.

Mother would sometimes ask me to, "Be more circumspect."

I would always reply, "I thought that was something they do to Jewish boys when they are eight days old."

The visit was short, stiff and formal. My Uncle Winston was a good friend and mentor to me, but he was an absolute slave to a truly complex system of protocol. The Bass family had more rules than the Sanhedrin.

Lunch was a salad again. Shrimp this time, and served once again in the breakfast room. After the cleanup, we took naps.

I don't suppose that nap-taking was actually obligatory in my family, but it was certainly deeply ingrained. My father gave everyone at his office an hour and a half for lunch. This was so they could, "Eat lunch, watch Jessie Helms (on TV), and take a nap." This practice was particularly pleasant on weekends after a few drinks.

∞∞∞∞∞∞

The next day, I took my family to church. Mother stayed home and busied herself in the kitchen preparing dinner. When my father was alive, Mother, who was an Episcopalian, had gone to the Presbyterian Church twice a year, and my father had done the same at the Episcopal Church. Mother had always felt sure that the Episcopalians were much more what God had intended than the Presbyterians and only made these semiannual concessions for the sake of "appearances". I can still hear her as she almost spat, "I *hate* Rally Day."

That Sunday, my father was no longer alive and it was not one of the special Sundays. She stayed home.

As the three of us approached the front door of the Church we were spotted by some of the older members who were standing out front. We were then swarmed by a covey of old ladies that had been contemporaries of my father. The men greeted us too, but the rush of smiling gray-haired females was warm, welcoming, and wonderful. Once again, I had the feeling of returning to the womb.

We sat in the family pew, arranged according to the protocol that had been in place for what was now four generations. I took my father's place next to the center aisle.

After the service, we made our way through what was almost a receiving line and went home for Sunday dinner.

My wife's family's midday meal was always called lunch, but at my Mother's table "lunch" was a small meal and "dinner" was a larger one regardless of the time of day that it was served. This was dinner.

Eastern North Carolina barbeque had an almost eucharistic status in my family. It was *always* served in a particular way, with particular condiments, a particular kind of cornbread, a particular beverage (lemonade) and a particular dessert (buttermilk pie). During my Mother's lifetime, I never saw the smallest variation in this ritual meal.

Now the service was different though. Instead being waited on at the table by orbiting servants, we fixed our own plates in the kitchen and carried them to the table, which was set in the formal way that I had grown up with. Best linen, china, silver, and crystal.

As I had at church, I again I took my father's seat. This was turning out to be quite a day.

After dinner we all pitched in for the cleanup. This was a new thing too. When I was growing up, I'd always had a lot of fun playing with my cousin Rob at his house. Over there, I could do things that I wasn't allowed to do at home. Like run around in my sock feet and wash dishes.

Then there was a short nap after which my family loaded the car and hit the road for Wilmington.

The visit had been a huge success. Everything had been more than pleasant. My mother told us that she would be visiting friends at Wrightsville Beach (near Wilmington) in three weeks and would like to see both us and our home while she was there.

∞∞∞∞∞∞

At my office, things were going well. I was enjoying the people that I was working with, and the field offices were in rural communities which once again put me in contact with the people that I had instinctively been drawn to all my life.

One of my first assignments was to assist in organizing and taking a detailed inventory of all of the company's equipment assets. This allowed me personal contact with all of the employees and agents across the entire sales area. I was "on the road" quite a bit and absolutely loved the process.

Because I was born in a small Southern town, people from other parts of the country sometimes assumed that I was familiar with farm life. Nothing could be further from the truth. I grew up in town and my family was involved in textiles. I knew about as much about farming as Oliver Douglas on the old TV show "Green Acres", but I was also just as fascinated by farming as he was.

Mother came to visit the beach as she'd planned and we were invited over to meet her friends.

Julia Peacock had been a childhood friend and college roommate of Mother's who had married a wonderful man from the nearby community of Fremont.

John Peacock was a prominent local farmer who had been drafted from the minor leagues to play baseball for the Boston Redsocks during the Great Depression. They were both warm and congenial people who my family grew to love. My son referred to John as "Mr. Redsocks".

Mother came to our house while she was in town. She had a meal with us, and gave us her seal of approval. We made plans for another visit to Tarboro.

My family was attending church services at First Presbyterian in Wilmington. Walking into that place was like stepping though a time portal. The services were exactly like those that I'd grown up with, which made me feel very much at home there.

The minister was Ed Hay, an older man who was a contemporary and friend of my father's older brother George. This gave us a family connection as well.

My duties in the fertilizer business continued to expand. The most significant of these new responsibilities came when the boss' son who was our computer operator left to take another job. His job fell to me.

In the 1970s, operating computers was still the mysterious province of "geeks" who wore horn-rimmed glasses and spent most of their time looking at their shoes. I honestly didn't know if I could do the job.

The machine was an IBM mainframe that the company used on a timesharing basis at night. It filled a good sized room which was equipped with special flooring, cooling and electrical equipment. It cost us $1,500 an hour to use, but was worth this high cost because of its tremendous computing power. It had 8k of memory.

I had two female employees who punched and verified the cards that were used to input programs and data to the machine, and would take trays of these cards on a hand truck over to the computer room at night for processing.

I liked this work. I liked being alone in the room with this giant machine and my thoughts. It was peaceful.

One Saturday in early December I was at home with my family, when my wife started to hemorrhage. She was eight months pregnant. I bundled her into the car and rushed her to the hospital, leaving Chris at home alone. I was in an absolute panic.

The doctors performed a Cesarean on my wife and our daughter Barbara was born.

I was with my wife in her hospital room when the doctor brought terrible news. Our child, a little girl, wasn't normal. In fact she was a very long way from normal.

The doctor said that she had been born with an open spine. The medical term that he gave us was myelomeningocele. He explained that this was the most severe type of spina bifida, and added that the common term for such children was "water head".

In very matter-of-fact terms he told us that she would have no chance whatsoever of having anything like a normal life. I know now that giving us this brutal truth unvarnished was the kindest thing that he could have done. It put both my wife and me into shock.

Dinah cried. I mumbled a "thank you", and told him that we would need to have some time to think before we could talk and ask questions. He understood perfectly. He was a superbly compassionate man, and knew that he'd given us much more than either of us could swallow.

He left, and I walked alone down to the hospital nursery to see my daughter.

What I saw was something horrible. A creature with a huge misshapen head lay in the incubator. It moved like a human child, had hands and feet like a human child, had the skin of a human child, but was not.

Then I saw her eyes. They were beautiful. She *was* a human child, and she was alive.

My heart broke, and I plunged into the abyss. Here was something unlovable that I had been given to love.

I stood there for a very short time. Probably not more than a minute or two, which was all that I could manage, then returned to my wife's room.

Dinah was terrified. She cried. She needed for me to be calm and to reassure her that everything was alright. The problem was that everything was definitely *not* alright. What she needed, I was powerless to give her. I was crushed.

I did the best I could with the situation, which was not very good, then left to go home and check on Chris.

Walking into the house, I first poured myself a very large shot of whiskey.

I then told my son that his mother was fine, but that his new little sister was very, very sick. I then had another shot of bourbon, made sure that Chris had something to eat, and returned to the hospital. Once again doing the best I could do at the time.

I don't have any clear recollection of the rest of that day. My wife saw the baby, there was another meeting with the doctor, and a telephone call to tell my mother what had happened.

I got a call from Winston, who gave me what I'd been unable to give to my wife.

"Crisis builds character," he said. He said a lot of other things as well that left me knowing I was not alone.

One thing I remember him saying was that a child like this could "ruin my life" if I let her. Eventually I would find that she would have the opposite effect on me.

∞∞∞∞∞

For the next five months, I moved as if in a dream. Time had lost its meaning. The experience was terrifying and painful, but the terms "fear" and "pain" really don't describe the state that I was in.

In Tibet, the Buddhists have the *Book of the Dead* which gives detailed instructions on what a person is to do when they are between lives. They refer to this time between lives as the Bardo realm. The in-between place you are when your old life has ended and your new life hasn't begun yet. This is where I was.

The doctors began a series of what would turn out to be twenty-one surgical procedures.

My wife came home from the hospital.

Winston called to tell me that the Episcopal minister in Tarboro was sending me a check for $3,000 from his discretionary fund to help us through the period. I think that the money actually came from Winston and he gave it to me by passing it through the church.

The minister and congregation of the Presbyterian Church in Wilmington gathered around us with expressions of supportive love.

My coworkers at the office were supportive too. However, the comfort offered by a couple of the more fundamentalist Christians was so disturbing that it drove me to sit down with a bottle of whiskey and a King James Bible to see if I could make sense of what was going on. I couldn't make sense of it, but this effort on my part would ultimately prove to be an invaluable part of my spiritual journey.

Some of my behavior during this period was impossible to understand. One morning, I returned from the hospital following one of the seemingly never ending string of surgeries.

I walked into the empty house, went to my bedroom and got a .22 Magnum revolver out of my dresser drawer. I then went to the garage and got a small puppy that we'd recently acquired. I took the dog out to the woods off River Road and shot it in the head. It began flopping around in its death throes. A second shot stopped that. I walked away and left it where it was.

Afterward, I could find no explanation for my actions. I wasn't particularly angry or fearful. It was as if something was moving through me.

Many years later I would get an answer to my questions about my actions in a dream, but at the time it was a puzzle. I kept quiet about it.

My work was suffering. I was obsessed with drinking and reading the Bible, but found no comfort there. The Church fellowship was unable to help. I had to have some relief.

Finally one evening while we were eating supper, the phone rang. It was the doctor telling us that our daughter's ordeal was over. It was a relief and a blessing.

The funeral was a private affair in Tarboro. The minister, my wife, and I were the only ones there. The service lasted about fifteen minutes which the minister could see was all we could stand.

After the funeral, back at Mother's house, we started discussions about moving back to Tarboro. Both my wife and I were thoroughly defeated, and the thought of moving back to my place of origin seemed natural and comforting.

∞∞∞∞∞

Nature is a wonderful force. In times of trouble She takes over in the most helpful of ways, and after a trauma moves in a compensatory fashion to balance, reassure, and heal.

Small examples of this were my waking up sometimes with a ripping hangover and finding myself with a magnificent erection. This was my body's way of reassuring me that I was ok. There was a lot of this kind of unconscious compensatory work going on.

I was doing a lot of deer hunting during this time, armed with a .45-70 Government rifle with very heavy handloads. I was hunting deer, but I was definitely loaded for bear.

Soon we found that my wife was pregnant again. It was a shock, but after we recovered from that, we found ourselves cautiously optimistic.

This time, the process proceeded normally and we were presented with a heathy baby boy. My second son was born. A third Adam.

Immediately after this, I got a call from a man named Brent Nash. Like me, Brent was a member of an old Tarboro family. He was a second-generation head of a local savings and loan association.

He was calling with the offer of a job at the S & L. I was taken aback, thrilled, and delighted. It seemed to be a perfect vehicle for my return to my roots and my place in the community.

Brent told me, "We don't make a lot of money here, but we live very comfortably."

I had known the Nashes all my life, and knew that "very comfortably" was very comfortably indeed. I accepted the offer without hesitation and without any discussion of, or worry about, the salary that I would receive.

A week later there was another call from Brent. He told me that he was going to have to rescind his offer. I was speechless. He soberly apologized, and assured me that the change was not of his doing.

It seems that a member of the Board of Directors had objected to my employment saying that it would result in "too much family" in the running of the organization. I thanked Brent, in as gentlemanly a manner as I could manage, for what he had tried to do and hung up.

Actually, my family connection to the Nashes was very distant. But it was there.

I was disappointed and very angry. I learned from one of my cousins that the offending board member was C. W. Wickham and promptly began to direct my disappointment and anger at him.

Clarence Wickham was not a native Tarborian. He'd been born in Richmond. He had later moved to Tarboro, where he had gone into the automobile business and made a success of himself. Now he was Chairman of the County Commissioners, was on a number of boards, and was a deacon in the Baptist Church. He moved in the best circles. He was generally respected, though not always liked, for his tough business acumen.

None of that mattered to me. I was furious.

Three days later, the phone rang again. This time it was Mr. Wickham. Fortunately, I was too surprised to say anything.

He was calling to offer me a job offer in his own business!

We arranged to meet at his office the following Saturday morning to discuss his offer in detail.

That Friday I took my family with me for a visit to Mother's, closed the deal on my new job on Saturday, and began making arrangements for the move home.

Chapter 7

The Homecoming
November 1975

There was a great deal to do, but once again things fell into place. I resigned from the fertilizer job, leaving on the best of terms. We put the house on the market with a good realtor and bid an emotional farewell to the church community in Wilmington.

I rented a two-bedroom apartment in a new complex in Tarboro, and my cousin Jack, Winston's son, volunteered to help with the move.

Chris traveled by bus to Tarboro a week ahead of the rest of the family so that his grandmother could get him started at his new school following the Thanksgiving holidays.

Mother took Chris for his first day of school and met the Principal, an elegant and dignified educator named Reginald Moss. Reggie was a black man.

When she told us about her experience, Mother was very pleased with how she had handled herself. "I did it!!" she said as if she'd scaled the North face of Everest. "I shook hands with him!" It was the first time in her life that she'd ever shaken hands with a black man.

When moving day came, Jack rolled up to the house in a big 18 wheeler van. We piled our worldly goods into the truck, filling it from the front of the trailer to the loading gate, and we were ready to go.

I rode with Jack in the big truck, and my wife drove the car with little Adam in a child's carseat beside her.

It was a clear November day and the miles passed quickly. By nightfall we had unloaded as many of our things as we could into the new apartment. The overflow, which were the things that we had no room for in the little apartment, would be stored at Mother's until we needed them again.

My wife and I took the master bedroom and Chris the smaller second bedroom. We converted a large walk-in closet into a nursery for Adam, taking out the shelves and hanging pictures.

The new job was exciting. I went from the fertilizer business to the automobile business, but continued to perform accounting tasks. I have had a lifelong interest in cars, particularly high-performance cars, so I slid into this new environment like a duck into a pond.

I was responsible for seeing to it that the paperwork for the car sales, including insurance, was completed properly. The dealership offered financing and insurance options and it was my aim to get customers to use as many of our "in-house" options as possible. I was paid a salary, plus commission on the finance and insurance options that I sold. I found that I was a good salesman.

Mr. Wickham's son-in-law was in charge of an affiliated company that sold mobile homes and I had the same duties for him too, with the same commission arrangement. Once again, I was making more money than I ever had.

C.W. Wickham was a tough man, and one of his primary management tools was fear. He kept his employees a little afraid of him.

On the other hand, he was one of the most honorable men that I ever worked for. He ran his business with a well-developed code of ethics that I found admirable.

For example, as Chairman of the County Commissioners, if the Sherriff's Department needed a new fleet of cars, they would not be getting them from his dealership. He was careful to keep an arm's length relationship between his professional and civic life.

∞∞∞∞∞

I found a suitable house for my family in the neighborhood that I'd grown up in, about two blocks from Mother's. It was a rambling one-story place which had been part of an old school building that had been located on the Town Common. The school had been broken up in the early 1900s and several houses made out of parts of the structure.

The place was comfortable and located on a large lot. It had a detached garage that fronted on an alley which ran down the middle of the block. The garage made a perfect workshop for setting up my ammunition-making tools.

I very much enjoyed working for Mr. Wickham, and being exposed to him and his circle of friends, who were men that I had known my whole life. Some of them would stop by the dealership in the afternoon to drink whiskey and talk politics. My enjoyment had to be at a distance, as I was an employee and could not be a part of his inner circle.

Soon after starting my new job, I was sent to Chicago for comprehensive training in automobile finance and insurance sales. The training went well, but during the trip I met and fell in love with a very powerful woman, who was a fellow student. She was from Texas. After I returned home, we began talking on the phone and writing letters to each other.

Although the affair had not been consummated physically, it put me in an untenable situation in my marriage. I was torn apart emotionally.

Nature stepped in and ended the conflict when my wife announced that she was once again with child. This ended the affair, but the relationship with my wife had been changed. My third son, Jack, would be born into a loveless marriage. The marriage would eventually end, but a lot had to take place before that could happen.

∞∞∞∞∞

My old back injury began to give me trouble. Twice I was forced to stay in bed for two or three days, unable to walk. Mr. Wickham told me in no uncertain terms to "get the problem taken care of", so I found myself scheduled for back surgery at the hospital in nearby Wilson.

When I awoke from the surgery, I found that I had no feeling in the lower part of my body. I was numb from the waist down. The doctor told me that he expected all or part of the feeling to return, which proved to be the case.

After three days I could tell that I was a boy again and was much relieved. A full recovery, however, was not to be. I spent three months in a hospital bed at home in my living room, and I walked with a cane for a year after that. When I left the hospital, the doctor told me that I could do whatever I wanted but, "...not to bend over and not to run." This was a very discouraging time. It seemed that what I wanted to do most was sit on my couch and drink whiskey.

Carrying this morose attitude back to work with me resulted in my situation there deteriorating as well. The company's sales manager, who had never been particularly fond of me, began to "get on my case". One evening I stayed late at the dealership after a company oyster roast.

The sales manager, Wickham's son-in-law, and I got into a three-way "pissing contest". Mr. Wickham, who had gone home for the evening, had to come back to the dealership to settle things down. After Mr. Wickham settled the dispute he headed home. A policeman noticed that his driving was erratic and he got a DWI sitting in his own driveway.

As a result of this indiscretion, being the moral man that he was, Mr. Wickham felt compelled to resign from his offices as deacon at the Baptist Church and Chairman of the County Commissioners.

Soon after this, he called me to his office and fired me. As with all his other interactions with me, this was done in a gentlemanly manner. "I know that this looks like a dark time," he said. "Just know that this is the kind of thing that will take you to a better place." This profound insight has never left me. It has proven to be a jewel of wisdom that has seen me through many other dark times.

∞∞∞∞∞

A week and a half-gallon of whiskey later, my cousin Sam called. Sam and his older brother, an investment banker who lived in New York, had undertaken a very bold business initiative.

They had managed to buy all of the stock of an old mercantile company that had been started by their great-grandfather, and were making a focused effort to radically expand the scope of the company's fertilizer division.

The old company had never had what could be called a real computer system. A part of the expansion plan was to update the company's information technology by installing a series of increasingly powerful IBM mid-range computer systems. Someone was needed to coordinate the upgrades, and my Wilmington experience both with information technology and the fertilizer business made me a perfect candidate.

I would not be working directly for my cousin Sam in my new position. Instead I would be reporting to Tom Cordle, his Chief Financial Officer. This turned out to be a very good thing for me because, unlike Sam whose moods could be mercurial, Tom was the same man every day and showed the same face to everyone he met. This made him much easier to work for than Sam. He was a very good boss.

Sam's great business talent was to find and hire the right person for a particular job, then to support him in his efforts. He had done this when he hired Tom Cordle. Sam was, and still is, one of the best businessmen I've ever met.

My new office was in Tarboro's downtown business district and was only four blocks from home. The walk was pleasant, and the situation allowed us to remain a one-car family. This was especially important since the new job represented a significant reduction in income, which in turn made it necessary for my wife to look for work outside of the home.

Thanks in part to our small-town network of friends, Dinah soon found work in the patient records department of the local clinic. The move into our new situation had once again been seamless.

∞∞∞∞∞∞

Life outside of the office was busy and full. My wife and I were included in the social activities of the "young upwardly-mobile" set in Tarboro. There were plenty of parties to go to, and we responded by giving plenty of them as well!

My love of outdoor sports, hunting and fishing, was well satisfied now. I became part of a cohort of male friends that enjoyed these pursuits and the drinking male camaraderie that went with it.

There were fishing trips to North Carolina's coast, which is a world-famous fishing ground. Sometimes we would stay at my family's cottage, which I now had access to, and fish in the surf or charter a boat for a day in the Gulf Stream. Other times we might take four-wheel-drive trucks to Cape Hatteras to use heavy surf rods when the Blues were running. There were also offshore big game fishing expeditions in my cousin Jack's 38-foot sports fishing cruiser.

My love of shooting sports flourished and my arsenal of weapons expanded to include high-velocity scope sighted rifles for hunting and target shooting. One of these rifles was a falling-block single-shot gun with a 24 power telescopic sight. I could only fire it effectively from a solid rest because the sight was so sensitive that I could see my heartbeat in it. When I had a sandbag to rest it on though, it was a hell of a tool. I could surgically remove a pigeon from the roof of a tobacco barn at 200 yards with no trouble at all.

There were plenty of shotguns and pistols to go with all the rifles. I was very heavily armed during this time and usually had some kind of gun within reach.

During the hunting season we were in the woods or fields a lot. We mainly hunted dove and deer, with an occasional duck hunt thrown in for good measure.

The Dixie Café, an old Tarboro institution, closed its doors for good and I managed to acquire their impressive array of commercial meat processing equipment, which I installed in my garage to process venison.

There was plenty of venison to process. Edgecombe County had become overpopulated with deer as a result of the Fish & Wildlife people overprotecting the herd for decades by allowing only the males to be taken. Now, in the summertime when the season was closed you could pull into a field and see thirty deer standing and feeding on the farmer's crops. Deer will eat most any young plant, including young tobacco plants. If you ever want to have a conversation with an irate farmer, find one that has just discovered that deer have been feeding on his tobacco crop. Pressure from these farmers had resulted in increased bag limits on deer and relaxed restrictions on hunting does. Not that my friends and I were overly concerned with the law.

My freezer was filled with fish and game. There were dinner parties with platters of dove and wild rice. There was venison sauerbraten. There was grilled wahoo served after a seviche appetizer. There was beer and wine and liquor and after dinner drinks served far into the night.

When the hunting season was over, my friends and I kept busy with various types of target shooting. Some of this was at target ranges, but a good bit consisted of riding around back roads in the county drinking beer and shooting pretty much any small animal we encountered.

There were several of us guys that enjoyed this pastime, but I particularly liked two of my men friends because of the dialectical contrast they presented.

The first was my old friend Henry Allred: the Snake Man. Henry remained a naturalist and a scientist. His big old house was filled to overflowing with telescopes, microscopes and books on science. There were snakes and turtles crawling on the floor, and once he coaxed a hummingbird to come inside. His office had petri dishes with cultures at various stages of development.

I really appreciated the fact that my son Chris (and later my other sons as well) could drop in on Henry unannounced on weekends. There, instead of looking at cartoons on television, he could look at the Orion Nebula through one of Henry's telescopes or examine microscopic animals swimming around with propellers on their asses.

I loved going there too! Henry and I would drink Old Grandad and talk about history, science, religion, and politics (mostly with Henry railing against "the bleeding-heart liberal idiots"). We'd listen to classical music and would keep at all of this until Valkyries were hanging from the ceiling. It was wonderful.

My other close friend during this time was Ben Gammons. The one word description of Ben would be "Big". He was a big man, well over six feet and well over two hundred pounds. He had a big, full, black beard. He wore a big hat. He drove a big red four-wheel-drive pickup truck, with big oversized mud grip tires and a big extra-capacity seventy-five gallon gas tank. And, he carried big guns; magnum rifles, pistols, and shotguns. He was Big Ben.

Ben was a few years older than me, and although we had similar temperaments, we had not known each other in high school. Ben had gone off to Georgia Tech, so while I was riding around Edgecombe County blowing up old cars with Eddie Patterson, Ben had been riding around Atlanta with my cousin Jack shooting fire hydrants with armor-piercing .30-06.

He and his family lived in a house that he had built for them with his own hands and that was heated with a wood stove which burned wood that he cut. When Ben stopped walking, pools of testosterone would begin forming at his feet. One of my sons sometimes referred to him as, "…that Hemingway-looking guy."

Ben was a natural hunter, just as my friend Charles from Kinston had been, but with some significant differences. He didn't hunt with dogs, other than retrievers. He was a consummate woodsman, and he was the best marksman that I have ever met, bar none. When I make this statement in the company of other men, some of them begin to puff themselves up and talk of their own exploits with firearms. They are wasting their breath. Ben Gammons was in a class by himself. We were walking through a small clearing in a woods one day when a pair of wood ducks flew across the clearing. Ben drew his four-inch barreled .44 Magnum S&W revolver and fired twice, picking them both out of the air before they could make it out of the clearing.

During deer season, Ben and I would hunt the W.S. Clark Farms. The Company farmed over 12,000 acres of land, mostly in Edgecombe County, making them one of the largest landowners in the State. My cousin Sam had given me permission to hunt the deer, telling me to be sure to leave the quail alone. The quail fell under the purview of Cotton Ruffin. Cotton was one of Sam's farm supervisors (he was in charge of growing the cotton) and the quail were part of Sam's "deal" with him.

Ben hunted deer with an elegant bolt-action .264 Winchester Magnum rifle that he'd gotten in Germany when the Army stationed him there. The scope sight was German too, and had an enormous objective lens that gave Ben a good sight picture on early mornings and on late evenings. In Germany, Ben had hunted by moonlight which was perfectly legal there. Now that he was home it was impossible to get him to agree that this practice was bad. I would sometimes be back at the truck, having finished hunting for the day, and hear the "boom" of the big Magnum. I then knew that we had a deer to clean.

Ben and I both killed a lot of deer. Some of his were taken after the legal hunting day had ended. This was just as illegal as what my friend Charles had done when we were together in Kinston, but it was a lot more sporting.

In the off season, Ben, Henry and I would go to the target range and give our rifles and pistols a good workout on paper targets and steel "silhouettes". The silhouettes were sections of steel plate cut in the shape of game animals. We'd set them up at ranges from 25 to 100 yards and knock them over with handguns. We'd sip beer and have a good time with this exercise until we got tired of it, then pile into Ben's truck and ride around the back roads of the county drinking beer and shooting animals out of the truck's windows. These redneck safaris were dangerous and illegal. They were also a lot of fun.

One day we were on a long stretch of dirt road when we saw an animal of some kind sitting in a field at a distance of about 250 yards. "What in the hell is that?" Ben asked.

"I don't know," I replied. "Kill it." This was my basic mindset at that time.

It turned out to be a groundhog. None of us had ever seen one before. Groundhogs were moving into our area. They came in force and were decidedly unwelcomed by the farmers. This provided us with a new kind of hunting.

As time passed though, a conflict developed between Ben the hunter and Henry the conservationist. Man is a predator, but there is something in man that sets him apart from other predators. As far as I know man is the only predator that will "make war" on other predators. Man will literally kill off the competition, thus increasing his own share of the game. Oddly enough, this characteristic seems to apply much more to the "civilized" white man than to the "primitive" native who is better able to live in harmony with Nature.

This "war-making" culture was the one that I had been raised in. In the 1930s, when my mother was a young woman, she would go to Friday night dances in the neighboring town of Rocky Mount. These dances were at the country club and were formal affairs. Tuxedos and evening dresses. Often Mother would go with Harvey McNair, a male friend who was a hunter.

Harvey would pick my mother up at her parents' house, bringing along a rifle and powerful flashlight. On the way to the dance Harvey would drive, and Mother would shoot feral cats. On the way back to Tarboro, Mother would drive and Harvey would shoot cats. They would keep score. It was part of the date, and part of how I was raised.

On my excursions with Ben, he would kill any hawk or feral cat that he came across. Having been trained the same way, I would do this too. The number of these animals that we continually encountered reassured me that they were anything but endangered species in our area.

Henry, on the other hand, would have none of this practice. He would shoot pigeons, crows, groundhogs and other pests, but objected vehemently to the taking of hawks and cats. Ultimately these differences proved irreconcilable, and our threesome dissolved. I remained friends with and admired both men, but ultimately came to Henry's point of view on conservation.

∞∞∞∞∞∞

At the office, the company's migration through the series of computers went smoothly. Technology has progressed with such disconcerting speed that all of the machines that I worked with then are now so outdated that they are nothing more than amusing relics.

At the time though, that was not the case. They were cutting-edge business machines and so was I.

I worked with a computer programmer to customize accounting software, and to custom write an inventory costing system that would accurately reflect the actual materials cost that went into each individual run of fertilizer produced at each of the company's production plants. The work was complex, amazing, and *fun!*

At the end of the month there were jobs involving large quantities of data that would take many hours to run. I would begin these processes in the afternoon and call my home telephone using an extension by the computer. My wife would answer the phone on my bedside table, then leave the phone off the hook on the table. I'd lay the extension at my end on the computer's printer and go home.

I would then have a few drinks, eat supper, watch TV and go to bed, setting my alarm for later on in the night. When the alarm went off, I would pick up the phone. If the printer had stopped, I would get dressed and go to the office to start the next part of the process.

My friends told me that I was regarded in the community as a "computer genius". Actually I was never that, but I saw no reason to correct this misconception.

At home, my situation *appeared* normal. My relationship with my wife was not unhappy, and my sons were growing. Chris was becoming an accomplished athlete, Adam was a precocious young boy, and Jack was Jack. He was a very sweet and loving child. He was also trouble brewing. Trouble that we could not see.

Denial is a very strange phenomenon. It is commonly thought that it is merely something that you are refusing to acknowledge, but in reality there is much more to it than that. It is something that you *cannot* see. An unthinkable thought. I could not see what was happening with Jack. Today I know that this blindness was a blessing and a manifestation of God's love.

My daily alcohol consumption was steadily increasing. For some years now I had been a daily drinker, which was the norm in my family, but the amount I was drinking had crept upward and restrictions on the time of day that it was ok to drink had disappeared. It was now normal to drink during the day on weekdays, and the morning drink was becoming more and more a manly thing to do. One day, the computer programmer that I was working with told me that I smelled like a liquor bottle.

Then, while my brother Ernest was in town for a weekend visit at Mother's, I went into a blackout while at a family dinner. When I woke up at home the next morning I couldn't remember what I'd done (to this day I don't know what it was). What I did know was that it had been something bad, and that I had pulled out a shotgun while I was doing it.

I quit drinking that morning.

Not being able to be sober and sit still, what I did next was to substitute a radical exercise regimen for the drink. After my back surgery, my doctor had told me that running was one thing that was definitely not good for me, but a running program was exactly what I now fell into.

At first I couldn't run, so I would walk as hard as I could for forty minutes every morning before work. After a couple of weeks or so I tried to run. Back pain stopped me and I went back to walking. I tried running again after another week, but had to back off again. I went through this cycle a couple of more times.

Finally I could run a mile. Then I could run two miles. Then five miles, then ten miles, and then twenty miles. I wasn't very fast, but I could run all the eight-minute miles anyone might want. I started running in 10K foot races on the weekends and training for a marathon. My obsessive nature had found a different focus.

The problem was that my body wasn't used to this level of stress. I begin to have problems with my knees whenever my mileage got to the forty-miles-a-week that my marathon training program called for.

The solution that I came up with was to abandon plans for the marathon, in favor of the triathlon. By adding swimming and bicycling to my running program, I found that I could work out as much as I wanted. I was running thirty miles-a-week, swimming three, and cycling a hundred and fifty. My weight went from the 220 pounds that I had been carrying during my couch potato phase, to a low of 136 pounds. I thought that I was extremely fit, and I did about a dozen triathlons. My resting heart rate was 52 beats-per-minute.

What I didn't then realize was that I had contracted exercise bulimia.

I wasn't throwing up like other bulimics, but I was just as sick. The workouts were the purge. Fortunately, "demon rum" came to my rescue. It began with my having a beer or two after the 10k races. That probably saved my life. After my body made contact with the old god, it didn't take too long for my alcoholism to progress. Soon I was drinking at home. Then I found that one of my favorite workouts was to drive over to the YMCA in Rocky Mount on my lunch hour. I'd swim a mile in their pool then drink a six pack of beer on my way back to the office. When I got back to work, I'd take a nap on my couch. It wasn't long before I began skipping afternoon workouts. Thus began my descent into the abyss.

∞∞∞∞∞

In the meantime, my mother's physical condition began to deteriorate. I talked with Winston about the situation and decided to sell the house on Trade Street and move my family into the Main Street house with Mother. Winston assured us all that this type of arrangement was an accepted norm in past generations, and pointed out that my parents had done the same thing with my mother's father.

At the time it didn't occur to me that this move invalidated my father's pronouncement that my wife and I would never live in the Main Street house.

We settled in. Tempus continued to fugit and I eventually found that I'd brought the installation of the computer system to a stage where I had worked myself out of a job.

I talked this over with Tom and Sam. Their suggestion was that I go into the credit administration part of the business. I gave it some thought, but decided that I'd had enough credit and collections work with General Electric to last me a lifetime.

Coincidentally, the Town of Tarboro was planning an upgrade of their badly outdated computer system. I hit on the idea of starting a computer time-sharing business and working on a consulting basis for both W.S. Clark's and the Town of Tarboro. I could, of course, add other clients as time went on.

After several months of negotiations I managed to reach agreements with both parties and found that I had become an "accidental entrepreneur".

Chapter 8

The Entrepreneur
May 1980

Success is as dangerous as failure...
                                    Lao-tzu

The first thing that I did as head of my new company was to hire Constance Moore away from Sam (with his blessing of course) to help me with my work. Constance was an attractive young woman who had worked under my supervision in data processing for W.S. Clark's the whole time that I'd been there. I knew her, knew what she was capable of, and would have been scared to try the new venture without her.

"I can pay you well," I told her. "But I can't do that and give you health insurance too. I don't have health insurance myself. I'm covered under Dinah's policy at the clinic."

"That's not a problem," she replied. "I'm covered under Shorty's (her husband's) policy where he works. I'd rather have the money anyway."

"Ok then," I went on. "You can have two weeks paid vacation a year and you can have all the sick time you need. Just don't get sick."

She nodded, smiling.

"You will work for me. Anybody else that we hire here will work for you."

"I won't have sex with you," she said firmly. "I save all that for Shorty."

We shook hands and began an amazing working relationship that lasted as long as the company did, and a friendship that is still ongoing.

I rented some office space from Sam on the first floor of one of the buildings that made up the W.S. Clark corporate headquarters. That floor was all rental space and we shared it with a law firm and an insurance business.

An electrical contracting firm made our new office ready, then a crew of six or eight strong men came from the fertilizer plant. They helped Chick Young, W.S. Clark's in-house carpenter, to move the thousand pound computer system from the second floor of the building next door, down the stairs, across the parking lot and into our space. The connections were made and our first client was up and running.

The Town's Public Works Department then descended on us and in a matter of days had run a coaxial cable under the street to where new terminals and printers were waiting at the Town Hall a block-and-a-half away.

We were in business, and I was working like I never before had in my life. I had to continue developing the W.S. Clark software platform and at the same time implement entirely new systems for the Town, which continued to run its old computer system parallel to ours until the changeover could be made.

Working for myself was a radical change. I was intensely aware that I could no longer walk up to someone else on payday, hold my hand out, and have them give me what I needed to live. It was like performing a high-wire circus act with no safety net. The instinctive fear was visceral. I can still remember it, but now it is a fond remembrance. It has become one of a series of such events that has taught me that those things that I'm most afraid of are portals of discovery that take me to a new life. I don't have any problem believing in reincarnation, because I've already been reincarnated so many times in this life.

Most of the work on the Town's platform was interesting and rewarding, but the mindset in the local government was much different from the corporate world that I was used to.

If a problem occurred in Tom and Sam's office, they would quickly move to fix the problem.

In the government office, however, the first order of business was always to find out who was to blame. Who had caused the problem? It seemed to me that if the building caught on fire, no one could evacuate until they found out who had started the fire. Learning to operate in this environment took some patience on my part.

Working with Joe Wheeler, the programmer that I was already using, I adapted several of our existing software systems, such as fixed asset management, for use by the government. We worked with the Director of Finance, who was a pleasant enough man, to make these systems operational.

In customizing the payroll system, one unusual requirement that the Director had was that on every payroll cycle, on every paycheck printed, we had to print the exact number of days that each employee had left to work before his or her retirement.

I found this to be a very odd way of looking at one's job. It was as if the point of working was to get it over with. Much like the idea that the purpose of living life is to get it over with and get to Heaven.

Ironically, this Director eventually committed suicide (by blowing his brains out I think) two weeks before his retirement. It was as if he had gotten to the top of the ladder he was climbing and found that it was against the wrong wall.

Joe and I custom wrote a utility billing system for the Town. Again, this was challenging and rewarding work for me. Computations for electric, water and sewer billing, as well as trash collection had to be developed and tested for a range of customer classifications. None of this was higher mathematics, but it was plenty complicated, and it needed to be done correctly.

The fly in the ointment on the Town contract turned out to be the accounting system. Joe Wheeler had customized accounting systems for many organizations, some with budgets much bigger that the Town of Tarboro, but talk as I might I couldn't convince the Town Manager to let us modify the system that we knew for their use. Instead, they insisted on using an IBM software system that had been developed especially for governmental accounting. This was a mistake.

The Town leased the software from IBM, but didn't spend the money necessary to train their personnel to use it. From day one this was a huge problem, and following their usual problem-solving protocol rather than fixing the problem, they looked for the person to blame. They quickly settled on me. My work with the Town became a nightmare that continued for the two years that remained on the contract.

∞∞∞∞∞

Salvation came in the form of a visit from my brother Ernest. In describing Ernest to people who haven't met him, I usually tell them that, "My brother is an internationally famous theoretical mathematician." This is true. He is a very talented combination biostatistician/epidemiologist, who manages huge, longitudinal, population-based public health studies. He travels all over the world "reading papers" on his work. His employers also encourage him to engage in consulting work.

Ernest and his family were in town one weekend visiting Mother. After lunch, the two of us took off to ride around the county, drink beer, and look for things to shoot. Ernest had an exciting idea!

"What we need to do," he said, "is to get involved in marketing research. Marketing research is the last branch of the statistical sciences that uses a table-driven approach to analysis. We need to bring advanced statistical techniques to the marketing research industry!"

His enthusiasm was contagious and, being filled with the Holy Spirit, I was soon onboard with the idea.

We formed a new company, The Statistical Analysis Center. Ernest knew of three female consultants, all named Catherine, who could and would use our services. We began to get projects at once.

Data collection (mostly in the form of telephone survey work) and management was done in Tarboro. Analysis and report writing was done by Ernest at his home in Winston-Salem.

Research computing is very different from business computing. In business computing, one might have files with huge numbers of records, but with relatively few variable in each records (say 375,000 records having 5 variables each).

In the type of research that we were doing, there would generally be a smaller number of records (say 1,000), but each record might have many more variables (say 200 in each record).

Additionally, it was necessary to keep numbers much more precisely for research purposes. Our business software typically kept numbers to 11 significant digits (for example $244,375,421.16). In research we used software that kept numbers in up to 64 significant digits, sometimes with many or most of these to the right of the decimal point (for example 7.8320423887553666).

Ernest was using the SAS (Statistical Analysis System) software product leased from the SAS Institute, in Cary, NC in his public health computing work, so we needed a computer that would run this software. The little IBM business computer that I was using wouldn't come close.

We set up a remote terminal in the Tarboro office that would allow us access to the computer that Ernest was using at Wake Forest University in Winston-Salem and began making plans for the installation of our own research computing system in Tarboro.

Ernest's department head was very gracious in accommodating us during this transitional phase.

Projects flowed in and our business began to expand. We were working primarily in the fields of banking and real estate development. Then Ben Gold, a researcher in the cable television industry, began to use our services and things took off. We were now doing projects for clients in New York, Atlanta, and out on the West Coast.

We needed more space and bought a three story office building that was a part of Sam's office complex and installed our own Digital VAX research computer.

Larger projects came in that included some political work and some work in the field of medical research. The medical research work proved to be the direction that most of our energy ultimately went into, but it took time to develop.

Ben Gold, the cable TV researcher based in Beaufort, NC, introduced us to Bob Schultz, another cable guy who lived in Asheville, NC.

I had several very productive telephone conversations with Bob, who then proposed to visit Tarboro to meet in person and have a first-hand look at our operation. I extended what was then the customary Southern invitation for him to stay at our home, and he accepted.

When the visit came, I settled him in the guestroom. We then took a stroll around town with my showing him the office and other points of local interest.

Bob was a Yankee Jew, a liberal, and a militant Zionist. I liked him at once. After supper with my family, we moved to the front porch to talk.

He began the conversation. "You know Adam, I've lived in North Carolina for six years now, and I've never actually met a Jesse Helms supporter." This was at the height of the North Carolina Senator's public exposure as the arch-conservative "Senator No".

I knew at once exactly what to do. "I can help you with that Bob," I said. "Oh *please* let me help you with that! I'm going to take you out for breakfast tomorrow morning." He agreed, looking intrigued at the prospect.

The next morning we went to the breakfast roundtable at Abram's Barbeque Resturant.

The Roundtable is an eternally existing archetype that predates the legend of King Arthur by millennia. I think it exists in all cultures and is, quite literally, a constellation of "the powers that be".

We found about a dozen (the usual number) men in attendance. I was not a regular at the meeting, but I knew everyone there.

"Good morning everyone," I began. "I'd like for y'all to meet Bob Schultz. Bob's in town on business. He's originally from Yonkers, but now lives in Asheville."

Zero Webb was the first to respond. "You must be one of those hemorrhoid Yankees," he said soberly.

"What's that?" asked Bob.

"One who comes down and won't go back up," Zero informed him.

Bob gave a delighted laugh.

I continued, "The reason I brought him here this morning, is that he tells me that he's lived in North Carolina for six years and has never met a Jesse Helms supporter."

Cliff Weeks was instantly aroused. "Well I'll tell you one thing!" he asserted. "<u>Everything</u> that Jessie Helms does is exactly right, and everybody else in the city of Washington, DC is a son-of-a-bitch!"

Bob and I sat down for breakfast and fellowship. Our relationship was cemented. We did business with each other until his retirement, and remained friends until his death. He is still with me in spirit.

At that time, Bob Schultz had a virtual monopoly on a particular kind of cable TV research that was both necessary for the industry and very profitable.

If you were the owner of a cable television network (or station), you were governed by a large and complex code of FCC (Federal Communication Commission) regulations that dictated what programs could, or in some cases must, be carried.

In the event that you wanted to deviate from these regulations, you would go to the FCC, where you would be referred to a gray-haired little old lady in the basement. When you explained what you wanted, she would say, "What you need is a significant viewing study."

"Where can I get one of those?" you'd ask.

"Bob Schultz is the only guy that does them right," she'd tell you.

You would then call Bob, who in turn would call us, and we'd go to work.

What Bob needed would be for us to locate about 110 people in a certain area, say Memphis TN, who *did not* have cable television, and who would agree to keep a TV viewing diary for a week. We would do this by telephone. We would then mail them a diary and a dollar bill to thank them for participating. Then we were done. They would mail the diaries back to Bob who would do the report. Occasionally, someone would challenge one of these studies, at which point Ernest would smile and blow them out of the water. My only real tasks were to go to the Post Office, get the checks, and put them in the bank.

The work poured in. My bank balance swelled, and my credit cards were paid off. I got a big new Audi 5000 automobile. The whole family got new wardrobes. The boys got new toys, and I got still more guns. I was trying to control my drinking and found I couldn't.

∞∞∞∞∞

As the company grew, our client base expanded. There was one of our original clients, however, that we were still doing business with. One of the three Catherines. Catherine Gibson.

Catherine was a beautiful, sophisticated woman who lived in Raleigh and operated her own consulting firm, which specialized in the banking and restaurant industries. She was divorced, having been married to a diplomat stationed in Thailand where she had lived with a houseful of servants and worked to further her husband's career. She was elegant and articulate and was *way* too much woman for a provincial Southern boy such as myself.

Her business, like ours, was thriving and we began spending a lot of time together, often with me being brought in to help with presentations to clients, such as bank boards. This was a lot of fun, since Catherine drank like I did. We would have a few drinks, make a presentation, and then go out for drinks and dinner afterwards.

Finally one evening down in Southern Pines, the dinner turned into dancing, and the dancing ended up in a motel room. This was a new experience for me. Not the sex, but the adultery. Up until then I, like President Carter, had often "lusted after women in my heart" but had never managed to actually act on it. Maybe at some level I was finally finishing what I had started with the woman from Texas on my trip to Chicago some years before.

Now that we were involved we began planning our next encounter. Catherine invited me for dinner at her apartment in Raleigh and I accepted. For this to happen, I would need help. Fortunately Henry Allred's older brother Frank was in town.

Frank was a sailor. He had served in the Navy, then joined the Merchant Marine as a communications officer. He was a hard-drinking womanizer who lived in an aura of mystery and romance. This aura was the result of his globe-trotting lifestyle, the over-the-top intelligence that he shared with his brother, the hypnotic effect that he had on women, and the persistent, unsubstantiated (but perfectly believable), rumors that he had robbed several banks in West Africa.

Frank agreed to help with my outing, which gave me a plausible excuse for being out very late at night. The two of us drove to Raleigh, I dropped Frank at the Foxy Lady Lounge where he could be adequately entertained, and completed my mission, picking him up afterward.

This experience taught me something very important about myself. I'm just not good at adultery. I had performed the act, but I found that I could not live with the duplicity and deceit that the adulterous lifestyle demanded. I was forced, and I do mean forced, to end my marriage.

This had nothing to do with any idea that I was supposed to marry Catherine, nor did it have anything at all to do with violating the Commandment against adultery.

As far as I know, I have never obeyed any of the Ten Commandments. I've really never considered myself subject to Biblical Authority, and I most certainly am not part of any covenant with the Christian God.

Whatever it is that makes these decisions for me is very powerful. It *will not* be denied. It is the same Force that compelled me to leave my Father's house in 1965.

I left home again.

Cousin Jack came to my rescue and I moved out to Robindale Farm. Robindale was a weekend getaway place owned by Uncle Winston and his wife Virginia. It was located about eight miles from Tarboro. As it turned out I was moving in just after a member of Aunt Virginia's family had settled his divorce and moved on. I remarked that we could rename the farm "The Virginia Bass Home for Displaced Husbands". She was not amused.

Chapter 9

The Profligate
April 1987

*Those who restrain desire, do so because theirs is weak
enough to be restrained...*
William Blake

Robindale was a 52-acre working farm that was part of the W.S.
Clark farming operation. It actually belonged to Aunt Virginia who
had been a Clark before she married Uncle Winston and became a
Bass. She owned a lot of other farms as well, all of which were
managed by my cousin Sam as part of the corporate farming
operation. I doubt if Aunt Virginia even knew where most of her
farms were.

In the early 1950s, Winston and Virginia had taken a rambling
pre-Civil War cabin on the place and remodeled it into a really nice
weekend home. There were three bedrooms and two living rooms
(one with really big windows for plenty of light and a panoramic
view).

There was a large kitchen with a 50's precursor to the Jenn-Air
grill. It was an oversized charcoal grill that was built into a counter
which wrapped around a central chimney. All this under a stainless
steel range hood with a powerful exhaust fan.

Outside there was a bunkhouse for young visitors, stables for the
children's horses, bridle trails, jumping courses, a buckboard, and a
horse-drawn wagon. If it snowed, there was even a one-horse open
sleigh (complete with chauffeur).

There was a pond with a canoe and a small motorboat. There was a skeet-throwing apparatus, grapevines, and a fig tree. And, there was a flagpole with both American and Confederate flags.

At the time of my residence there, the horses and associated paraphernalia, including the chauffeur, were gone. That didn't bother me a bit. I was there by myself, and as a place to be exiled to it was amazing. I knew exactly how Brer Rabbit felt.

I was free of the bonds of matrimony, living in palatial bachelor's quarters, and was a partner in a booming business. I once read somewhere that the only time that the god Dionysus over-indulged and got drunk, he turned into a jackass. The same thing happened to me.

I had been married to Dinah for over twenty years, which meant that I hadn't had a date since 1965. Even though I began seeing Catherine Gibson, I figured that I still had a lot of catching up to do on top of that. I soon learned that the rules of the dating game were much different that they had been in 1965. I liked the new rules.

Women, some of them "good" girls from "good" families, would come out to the farm, walk into the house and look around, then just start taking their clothes off.

My drinking went off the scale. I would come home from the office, fix a drink, and put on some music. Then I'd put my feet up in the sunken living room and look out over the pond. All of my troubles would dissolve. The more I drank, the smarter I got. One morning I woke up at 2:30 am sitting in my car in the middle of a cornfield. I couldn't remember how I got there.

∞∞∞∞∞

The relationship with Catherine was stormy. I was badly overmatched and was trying to please her but couldn't seem to get it right. The harder I tried, the worse things got. This relationship dynamic would be repeated in my life after Catherine and it would only be then that I would be able to understand and appreciate its deep spiritual significance. Only then could I be truly grateful to the Goddess for Her gifts to me.

Sometimes we saw each other in Raleigh, sometimes at the farm. We took some trips to the beach together. We fought. She won.

Catherine said that I needed contact lenses and I got contact lenses. She hurt my feelings about my wardrobe, so I drove over to a men's fine clothing store in Rocky Mount.

"My girlfriend says that I dress like somebody's first husband," I told the clerk.

"I can help you fix that," he replied. And he did.

Soon my suits were of the best quality. My shoes were hand-sewn. My shirts had to be custom made for me, since my sleeve length was 34½ and that couldn't be bought off the rack. My ties were silk, my underwear Egyptian cotton. My socks were nothing like "what Daddy used to make".

I looked like a million dollars, but it was all smoke-and-mirrors. No substance.

A woman friend said to me over dinner one night, "Adam, you really are a class act." She had no idea how right she was.

∞∞∞∞∞∞

At the office, the nature of our business was changing. We developed a statistically complex customer satisfaction tracking package for a major telephone company, which we ran on our computer for them on a contract basis.

We became involved with tracking patient cohorts in NIH (National Institutes of Health) funded studies for the Bowman Grey School of Medicine (Ernest's crowd) in Winston-Salem.

We got a contract to provide data entry services to a major pharmaceutical company based in Research Triangle Park.

We contracted to provide recruitment and follow-up for ongoing dietary intervention studies on cancer patients for Duke University. These studies required our staff to be trained on the most complex computer-assisted interviewing software package that I ever encountered.

We successfully recruited over 3,000 post-menopausal women, who were not taking estrogen, to participate in a phase-three clinical trial for an Atlanta-based pharmaceutical company.

Research in the cable television industry continued to thrive and the head of one cable network visited us in Tarboro.

Soon we had outgrown our three-story building and had to rent additional space from Sam.

∞∞∞∞∞∞

After the separation, Dinah hired a well-known and much feared divorce lawyer from Greenville. He told her that under no circumstances should she move out of the Main Street house, so she dug in like a tick and cohabited with her soon-to-be ex Mother-in-law. It's hard to imagine a more awkward situation, but my mother had the constitution of an ox. The battle was on.

I had as spectacular a divorce as anyone could want. I hired a local friend, Tom Brady, to represent me. Tom later told me that it was my case that convinced him not to do any more divorce work.

I don't know how many times we went to court, but it seemed as if I was always either going to, or recovering from, a court appearance. Tom kicked the hired gun from Greenville around the courtroom so many times that Dinah finally fired him and hired a local guy. There was plenty of drama.

Dinah broke into my office one night (using a key that she still had) and used *my* photocopier to make copies of some of my correspondence from a girlfriend that made reference to some jewelry that I had given her. She put the letters back and produced the copies as evidence in court.

I counterpunched by hiring a private detective to follow her to a Rocky Mount "meat market" bar where she met a man. The detective then followed them to a friend's house, where they spent the night. We called the detective as a witness.

The process seemed to go on forever, and even when the divorce was granted, there was still the question of the division of assets. In the North Carolina legal system this part of the process is called "Equitable Distribution". This name for this proceeding was doubtless thought up by someone with a very macabre sense of humor.

∞∞∞∞∞∞

Meanwhile, back at the farm, my social life was keeping pace with the rest of the chaos. I began spending time with Steve Hardee, another friend of many years.

Steve is a very attractive man. He was then living in Tarboro, but managing family farms around the nearby town of Leggett. He looks like a big Australian cowboy. Curly blond hair and shining blue eyes. He's another of my male friends who's a good bit bigger and stronger than I am.

I had really gotten to know Steve when he was married to his first wife Sue, who had been a friend of Dinah's. I hadn't spent any real, personal time with Steve, but Dinah and I were invited by them to go down to Belhaven to visit some of Sue's family there. Belhaven is a charming town on the Pamlico River, east of Washington, NC.

After we had accepted the invitation, a couple of people warned me about Steve. "You need to watch out for him," they said. "Going to Vietnam really messed him up. He was fine before that, but you need to watch him now!"

The girls went on down to Belhaven that Friday morning, and Steve picked me up after work in his truck to go down and join them. We each opened a beer before the truck left the curb, and were on our second one by the time we'd crossed the river bridge four blocks away.

Not knowing what else to talk about, I dove right in. "I understand you were in Vietnam," I said.

"I loved it!" he replied. "Riding around in helicopters, shooting people. Just like in the movies."

By the time we reached Belhaven two hours later, we'd become friends for life. He is as fine a man as I have ever known.

Now he was married again, and his wife Elizabeth is on the list of my top five favorite women of all time. The three of us began taking long rides in the country in Steve's truck, with Elizabeth doing most of the driving and Steve and I doing most of the drinking. This was not about shooting, though there was a gun in the truck. It was about laughing, talking and having fun.

We'd stop at a country store, buy a couple of beers apiece for Steve and me and drive on. When they were gone, we'd stop at another store and do the same thing again. We had no destination and covered a lot of miles just wandering around that way.

Steve said that he knew a girl that I ought to meet. He and Elizabeth came for dinner at the farm, bringing the incredibly beautiful Virginia Bundy with them.

Virginia, who lived in nearby Greenville, was from a large Gates County farming/logging family. She was just plain gorgeous. Slim, with beautiful brown hair that reached halfway down her back, and brown eyes. Her voice was low and soft and as smooth as silk.

102

"Back in Gates County, everyone calls her 'Little'," Steve had told me. "She has a brother that they call 'Big'. I think she'd really like for you to call her Virginia though."

I was perfectly willing to call her whatever she wanted to be called.

The four of us had a very nice evening, and the Hardees offered to have Virginia and me for dinner at their place the following weekend.

The following Saturday I picked Virginia up at her apartment in Greenville. I then stopped at a convenience store to get some beer for the drive to Tarboro. Virginia stood staring at the beer cooler.

"What would you like?" I asked.

"Scotch," she replied.

That night turned out even better than the first one, and there were many more to come over the next couple of years.

∞∞∞∞∞

At about the same time, I got involved with another girl that I met in Charleston, SC when I was down there running in the Cooper River Bridge Run. The Bridge Run is a 10K foot race that is conducted (of course) over the Cooper River Bridge. In addition to being a serious competitive event, it is also a huge social event and a Chamber of Commerce initiative with thousands of participants.

Having met this girl, Sallie Campbell, in a bar after running the race, I began a long-distance relationship with her.

The trip from Tarboro to Charleston was a five-and-a-half hour marathon driving as fast as I dared down Interstate highways. Not my idea of fun, but the Spirit made me willing.

I would get out onto I-95, set the cruise control on 80, open the sunroof, and settle in. On some of these trips I would then be passed by a small convoy of exotic cars. Porsches, BMWs, Mercedes, and so on. They would blow right by me like I was standing still, doing well over 100 mph. I would fall in behind them and follow along. They had radar detectors.

The protocol was for one of them to take the lead and assume the greater risk of being ticketed. After some period of time, he would drop back and another driver would move up and take a turn. This gentlemanly behavior appealed to me greatly and I thought it would be rude of me not to equip myself to take a turn in exposing myself to arrest as well. I bought a radar detector and became one of the outlaw gang. I found that by doing this I could cut about an hour off the trip. I was very pleased.

On one of these expeditions, I left on Thursday instead of Friday in order to accommodate some plans that Sallie had to start her weekend early. The traffic on I-95 was light and there was no convoy to join, but I opened the sunroof on the Audi, put on a Jimmy Buffet tape and let-er-rip anyway.

I crossed into South Carolina with beautiful weather and the speedometer ranging between 110 and 120 mph. As I entered Sumter County, I glanced to my left and saw a South Carolina State Patrol car in the highway median. I stood on the brake, but it was too late. The radar detector sounded its useless warning and I saw the patrolman's head snap up from his screen. Our eyes locked. We both knew he had me. I took my foot off the brake and began coasting to a stop as a cloud of dust erupted from under the accelerating patrol car.

The patrolman was a little bantam-rooster guy and he was hopping mad. Literally so mad he could hardly stay on the ground.

"Mister!" he shouted red-faced. "What do you think you're doing? A hundred and eight don't get it in this State. Where are you going?"

"I'm headed for Charleston," I replied.

"Let me see your license and registration," he barked. I handed them over. "What's so important in Charleston?" he asked.

"I've got a date," I said soberly.

"Maybe I ought to meet this girl," he said, somewhat mollified. Then he continued, "Here's what's going to happen. If you don't give me $115.60 in cash right now, you are going to the Sumter County Correctional facility."

I didn't have that much cash on me. All I had was my credit cards and a trunk full of imported beer, which I wasn't going to mention.

"All I have are credit cards," I said meekly.

"Cash!" he snapped back. He was barking again.

He took me back to his patrol car and we talked. He asked me where I lived and what kind of work I did. I explained all that as best I could, and he calmed down. Finally he said, "Ok. I'm going to let you mail the fine in, *or* you can come back down here and defend yourself in court, in which case we'll lock your ass up." That was that.

The weekend was a great one. Arriving back at the Farm exhausted and hungover on Monday, I dropped my luggage in the kitchen and walked into the living room. I heard a hissing sound and saw a good-sized black snake going down the window sill down in the sunken part of the room. I started toward it, thinking I'd catch it for the boys to take to school to show their classes.

Now the hissing was *very* loud, and I saw a second snake going into one of the bedrooms. I turned around to get out of the house and saw a third snake going into the kitchen. I got outside as fast as I could.

I know now that the snakes were hallucinations that resulted from my having had too much fun, but at the time they were real. I called my friend Perry Jenkins who came out with three Jack Russell terriers. Jack Russells are snake-hunting dogs. They went through the whole house but found nothing. Still, I was so shaken that I kept a revolver loaded with shot cartridges on my bedside table for the next few weeks and carried it with me when I got up to pee at night.

That spectacular speeding ticket did nothing to slow me up. I got a couple more tickets in rapid succession that, while not quite as fantastic, were enough to cause me to lose my driver's license for 90 days. This didn't affect my love-life as the girls that I was seeing then seemed to like it.

My automobile insurance was cancelled too. The only company that my agent was able to find that would agree to insure me was Lloyd's of London. When he gave me the bill for the premium, he said, "Adam, when we're buying Christmas presents for our customers this year, you're on the list for the ham."

∞∞∞∞∞

In time, the courts granted my divorce. As my lawyer had predicted, nobody got what he wanted. Dinah was getting alimony, but the amount was much less than she had imagined, and I was required to make child support payments that were a lot bigger than I had expected.

Dinah moved out of the Main Street house to a rental place in another part of town, pillaging my family's heirlooms on her way out. I returned home from my delightful exile. My sons had come to think of the Main Street house as their home. My son Chris was away at college now and doing well at it, but Adam and Jack spent most of their time with me. My mother provided most of the adult supervision while I continued to race at an ever-increasing rate of speed down Blake's "road of excess".

An inebriated afternoon in Greenville resulted in a new BMW. That was a really fast car. I touched 135 on the way home from the dealership with it, and that was only fourth gear.

A similarly inspired trip to a Rocky Mount gun shop to get shotgun shells for the opening day of dove season led to fine new shotguns for Adam, Jack and myself.

There was a continual inflow of new clothes, and plenty of wine, women and song. My mother's only comment on all this carrying on was, "You're painting with a mighty wide brush."

The post-divorce courtroom proceedings with my now ex-wife were an ongoing hard-fought battle. Dinah had spent most of our twenty-plus year marriage as a dependent spouse. She was entitled to half of all of our assets which included half of my half of the business. But what was that worth?

Her attorney argued that the business was a viable, going concern. My attorney argued that it was basically worthless as I really couldn't sell it for anything unless the deal included my personal ongoing participation. The only value that the business had, apart from used computers and office equipment, was me.

This "war" lasted for eight courtroom appearances, some of which took up to a half-day of court time. I showed up for one of these hearings carrying a double-armload of files and ledgers and sat down next to an attractive woman in the courtroom gallery. "All that for one wife?" the woman asked. We began talking and I learned that divorce court can be a good place to meet interesting females.

After firing the "hired gun" divorce lawyer from Greenville, Dinah had retained a local man, Marvin V. Horton, Esq. to represent her. Marvin, whom I have known all my life, is an archetypal Southern lawyer. An intriguing combination of Greek orator and riverboat gambler, his courtroom presence is the stuff of local legend.

Most of the work on Dinah's case was handled by a junior partner, but midway through the campaign, there was a motion that a national accounting firm, McLaren & Pullen, be retained for a second time to make another attempt to penetrate the company's books and make a determination on the value of the business. Their last visit had cost us about $15,000, so we were more than ready to resist the motion. For this event Marvin made a personal appearance, which I considered high praise.

After getting me on the witness stand and having me sworn in, Marvin began to probe. His questions about my accounting practices were expert and went on for about 30 minutes, but he was unable to bring anything new to light.

"I'm not an accountant," I finally told him.

"It seems to me that you could teach accounting," he replied and had no further questions.

Tom Brady's summary of our position to the judge was brief and to the point, "Your Honor, in making this motion, we feel that the plaintiff is endeavoring to shift an unfair portion of the cost of this litigation to the defendant, and we object," he said.

Then Marvin stood up and delivered, with powerful eloquence, exactly what he was being paid for.

"Your Honor, while Mrs. Thomas has been out of the marketplace for several years now, Mr. Thomas on the other hand is a man of great acumen, perhaps even genius, and we feel that she needs all the help that she can get in resolving this matter."

The judge's head turned to look at me. I smiled and shrugged.

Leaving the courtroom after the hearing, I walked directly to the office of one of my girlfriends. "What could I do?" I asked her, howling in laughter. "There I sat! Helpless in the face of truth!"

My brother Ernest had some note pads printed up for my office: From the desk of Adam Thomas: "*A man of great acumen, perhaps even genius.*"

What fun all that was!

Chapter 10

The Socialite
April 1989

I refuse to join any club that would
have me for a member.
                                    Groucho Marx

One fine spring morning, I took all three of my sons to Rocky
Mount so that all of us could update our spring wardrobes. The
downtown men's shop was the same one Catherine Gibson had
driven me to a couple of years back. I was a good customer, and
everyone there was glad to see me.

I had the boys fitted for new sport coats and slacks while I was
measured for custom tailored eveningwear (dinner jacket and tux).
After we'd finished our business, I stuck my head in the women's
department, which was up a short flight of stairs, to say "hello" to
Deann Smith, a woman who I knew was dating Ben Gammons (Ben
was now a widower). She had a surprise for me.

"Ben and I would like for you to meet that cute little blond over
there."

I turned and saw Brenda Smith (no relation to Deann) for the
first time. She was a vision. Beautiful enough to make me stammer,
with sparkling blue eyes and Southern Belle charm. She had a local
accent and was obviously what my mother called "our kind of
people". I learned that she was working in the women's shop on
Saturdays to "help out" the owners. Her beauty and the way fine
clothes looked on her made her a great help indeed. She was a
walking model of what they were trying to sell.

I was badly shaken, but managed to get her phone number and permission to call her, which I did after supper that evening.

The following Saturday night, Ben and I cooked dinner for Brenda and Deann at the Main Street house.

Dove, wild rice, and asparagus; with lemon ice and chocolate cookies for dessert. It went perfectly. I was in my family home and was the embodiment of the manner of living that had been so deeply ingrained in me by my mother's never ending coaching in "the way things should be done". Brenda never had a chance.

The affair was so hot it sizzled. We began seeing each other every day, and daily love notes that Brenda was getting from another suitor (the head of Marketing for Hardee's Food Systems) were thrown in the trash unopened.

One evening, after three weeks in this chemical furnace, we were fixing a romantic dinner for two at Brenda's parents' weekend cabin near Spring Hope, NC. We'd had a couple of bottles of wine and were beginning to lose interest in the dinner that was almost ready.

Brenda got up from the couch where we were sitting, and walked across the room. When she bent over to take something out of the oven, I proposed. Laughing about this later, I told Ben, "I just couldn't help it!"

She accepted with no hesitation whatsoever and I found myself engaged to marry someone that I hardly knew. When I eventually had time to think soberly about what had happened, I felt a good bit of fear. I reasoned however that in the words of the old song, "It's too late to turn back now." I pressed bravely forward.

I woke up the following Saturday morning, had breakfast, which included three Bloody Marys, and drove over and picked Brenda up at her parents' house to go shopping for an engagement ring. We drove directly to Bailey's Fine Jewelry in Rocky Mount.

When we walked in the door, one of the salesladies exclaimed, "Brenda!" She came right over and there were hugs and kisses. When she heard why we were there, she began to titter.

Brenda looked carefully at everything in the showcase, but couldn't find anything that suited her. The saleslady then said, "Let me call Lois." Lois, who was the store manager, came over. Once again there were hugs, kisses, and tittering. I was getting nervous.

"Can you draw me a picture of what you want?" asked Lois.

"Yes!" said Brenda, and using a pencil and a scratch pad that was on the counter, she did.

"We have that!" exclaimed Lois. "It's in the vault." This made me *really* nervous.

Lois went into the back of the store.

Out came the ring, and out came Clyde Bailey, the President of the company. There was still more hugs, kisses and tittering. I badly wanted to be someplace else.

The ring was magnificent. A perfect emerald-cut 6 carat diamond solitaire set in a platinum band, with two diamond encrusted wedding bands that would bracket the engagement ring after the ceremony.

"Take it with you," Clyde said. "Keep it over the weekend. Give me a call next week and we'll talk about it."

We left the store with me knowing that I'd already bought the ring. Brenda and I drove around Rocky Mount, her drinking wine and me drinking beer, showing the ring to her friends and family.

They all loved it. What was there not to love about it?

When I got settled at the office on Monday, I called my new friend Clyde to see how much money I'd spent.

$35,000.

∞∞∞∞∞∞

During the next month, three things happened. First, a New York TV network declared bankruptcy. We had just finished a nationwide survey project for them. We would not be paid.

Second, a long-term client based in Washington, DC went out of business. There would be no new projects from that source.

Third, a change in FCC regulations reduced the flow of work from Bob Schultz from a river to a trickle.

The effect of these three events happening at a time when the company's overhead was at an all-time high, and the cost of my own lifestyle so far beyond reason, was disastrous. I didn't handle the situation well. Not well at all. Pride and arrogance that were the result of my grossly over-inflated ego made it impossible for me to back down from anything.

Plans for a grand wedding, to be followed by a honeymoon in Athens, moved forward.

I rented a very nice four-bedroom brick house about a block from the Main Street place and Brenda began "nesting".

The new residence would be filled with all new furnishings in keeping with her tastes. Shopping trips that ranged from one end of the State to the other resulted in newly acquired goods arriving by the truckload. Brenda's son Jeff would be living with us, as would Adam and Jack, so a new car was bought for use by the boys. There was a lavish celebratory party to welcome the new bride to the community. All of this was on top of what had already been insane extravagances on my part.

By the time that the wedding actually took place things were already unraveling. I didn't have enough cash for payrolls, so I would borrow five or ten thousand dollars from one of my friends "for a few days". The following week, I'd do the same thing from another friend and use the money to pay back the first friend.

I stopped paying utility bills, and started paying cut-off notices.

These occurrences were but the leading edge of a coming holocaust.

∞∞∞∞∞∞

The wedding was a lovely, formal, ceremony at Thomas Memorial at noon on a beautiful Saturday. The reception that followed was a "big tent" affair at the Blount Bridgers House (Tarboro's answer to the Taj Mahal) with lavish food and drink, and refined music provided by a string quintet made up of "symphony wives" (wives of musicians in the North Carolina Symphony).

I was miserable and bad-tempered. What I really was was afraid, but I couldn't acknowledge the fear, so it came out as anger. As soon as I reasonably could, I grabbed Brenda and left on our honeymoon.

I had managed to evade the trip to Athens, and we went instead to Bald Head Island. Bald Head is an exclusive island just south of Wilmington. It's a true island, meaning that there is no bridge to the place. A passenger ferry took us over.

A sign by the boarding ramp announced, "The Recession Ends Here". I began to feel a little nauseous. We boarded on foot. There are no automobiles on Bald Head Island (other than service vehicles).

On the island everyone got around on golf carts, and we found ours. We loaded our luggage and started for the cottage that I'd rented. Enroute, we passed a cart coming in the other direction that had a Mercedes emblem affixed to its front. The owner had apparently been unable to leave his identity behind on the mainland. I then felt really nauseous.

We were there for a week, and in that time I found no one on the island, including my new wife, that I had the slightest desire to get to know better.

∞∞∞∞∞∞

Back at home, I had become a drowning man. A drowning man is flailing around grasping for something, anything, to keep from going under. If you get close to a drowning man, he'll pull you down with him. He'll kill you. Nothing personal, he just will.

One of my brothers-in-law called. His business, like mine, was experiencing "temporary cash flow problems". We started kiting checks. Check kiting is an old practice in which you write a check on one account, say for payroll, then write another check on a different account to cover the first. In today's world, this will no longer work because of the speed at which bank transfers occur, but at the time it was possible to use multiple bank accounts to keep large sums of money in cyberspace. This money was called "float". The practice was called a felony.

Checks were bouncing and bills were unpaid. June rolled around and the time came for the Great Vacation of '91. I reserved a condominium at Wrightsville Beach for a week.

Brenda and I left Tarboro driving the BMW. I had decided to take that car, since there were four payments due on it and if I'd parked it anywhere and left it for a week, the bank would have repossessed it. We drove to the beach where I wrote a bad check for the condo rental. We then went to the condo where we found a note waiting for us. The note informed us that my stepson Jeff (who had by this time been thrown out of boarding school for drugs and was living at Carolina Beach) was in the New Hanover County jail, charged with larceny.

We drove over into downtown Wilmington where I wrote another bad check to a bail bondsman to get Jeff out of jail. Writing bad checks to bail bondsmen is *not* a good idea.

I then contacted a well-known local attorney that I was familiar with from my previous experiences in Wilmington. After writing him yet another bad check, I went back to the condo and had a drink.

114

Monday morning came and we took Jeff for a First Appearance in court. The three of us sat together and waited for our turn before the judge. There was a short recess, and I used the time to go to a payphone in the hall. I called the office to try to figure out what do to about the bad checks. The IRS had seized my bank account.

∞∞∞∞∞

Back at home, my disposition moved from being merely unpleasant to something else. I became dangerous.

I came home from work one day, having been drinking since lunchtime. The bank had closed one of my accounts that morning because of the check kiting. It was the payroll account. I would probably have been arrested had I been doing business anywhere other than in my little hometown.

My son Adam said the wrong thing to me (actually, anything he might have said would have been the wrong thing), and I began chasing him through the house beating him as hard as I could on the back with a broom handle.

Christmas was coming, and in spite of my attempts to get Brenda to understand our situation, the house started filling up with Christmas presents.

Brenda bought a beautiful live tree and decorated it with elegant ornaments of silver, crystal, and porcelain. No one but her was allowed to touch it. I ended up with a $1,500 Christmas tree.

I threw the tree into the yard in a drunken rage. She followed it out and sat in the wreckage like a small child with a broken toy.

The following February, we were invited to a huge party in Rocky Mount to celebrate the opening of a new office. One of Brenda's friends had a successful physical therapy business and was moving into elegant new offices in the Boice-Willis Clinic.

I came home after work, already pretty drunk. I had been a daily drinker for some time now. I didn't seem to be able to stand being sober.

I shaved and showered, then dressed myself in my tuxedo. Brenda was at work on her side of the bathroom with her preparations. Looking at myself in the mirror, I thought, *I really can't keep doing this. Forever is too long. Please God kill me!*

We went to the party, where I stood by myself thinking. Once again, I was at a place where there was nobody that I had the least interest in talking to.

I don't remember leaving the party, but somehow found myself at an after-party at the hostess' home. I don't remember much of that party either. I do remember looking at an asshole of an architect leaning against the mantle in the living room. I wanted to pull his head off.

Then I woke up at home. It was morning.

Images came of sitting in my car in the hostess' driveway and my fist hitting Brenda in the face.

I jumped out of bed and almost fell. I was still drunk and was very disoriented. I felt my way downstairs to the kitchen and fixed a pot of coffee. I had no idea what to do next.

I took a cup of coffee and walked to look out of the living room window. The car was there, so I had driven home.

I walked through the house. I was there alone. I was in bad trouble. I knew that if I didn't do something, I was going to be arrested. But what could I do? Who could I go to?

I thought of calling the Mary Frances Center, which was a local treatment center for drug and alcohol abuse, but decided against that. The place was too expensive. As my mother would have said, "It costs like blue smoke."

Also, I had a cousin that worked there and I didn't want to get involved with her right then.

Then I thought of Stacey Fountain.

Stacey "Wild Thing" Fountain, was a local legend who lived out in Leggett. He'd gotten his nickname in college and had maintained and enhanced it when he came back home to manage the family farms with a life of splendid extravagance.

It was said that he hadn't had a drink in nine years. I didn't really believe that, but he was certainly more approachable than the treatment center or the church.

I called Stacey and he came right over. This immediate response was in itself uncharacteristic of him. I felt that something had changed in his character. We talked for a couple of hours. He told me what I needed to do and I did it.

"Adam, this doesn't have to be a bad thing," he said. "In fact it *could* turn out to be the best thing that ever happened to you." This statement turned out to be prophetic.

I went to an outpatient treatment program for alcoholism in Greenville, and thence to Alcoholics Anonymous.

∞∞∞∞∞∞

C.G. Jung, in his autobiography *Memories, Dreams, Reflections*, recounts the satisfaction that he got from his reading of Goethe's *Faust* in finding that there were people other than himself who, "…saw evil and its universal power, *and – more important – the mysterious role that it played in delivering man from darkness and suffering.*" (Italics mine.)

I was to be a recipient and experiencer of this Mystery and to find other teachers, such as William Blake ("…But in the Book of Job, Milton's Messiah is call'd Satan") who had had the same realization.

This didn't happen in one day though. It was to take years of the most painful work there is.

The main obstacle that I would have to overcome was the idea of God that I had been given growing up in a Christian Church. This

God is not Whole. Actually, he is Whole, but he is not fully conscious. He hasn't managed to deal with the problem of His own rejected Son.

I'm not talking here about the idea of God that any one individual might have, but rather the Christian God that lives in the collective psyche. That God is very much alive (Nietzsche was "dead wrong" about that) and very powerful. He's just not fully conscious. Not aware of his own darker, or shadow, side. It is my calling to help Him with that.

∞∞∞∞∞

I am not one of these people that walked into AA and found it wonderful. Just the opposite. I got to AA the same way that Jonah got to Nineveh, against my will, and in the belly of the whale. I didn't like it and didn't want it.

In the book *Alcoholics Anonymous*, Bill Wilson wrote that, "Circumstances made us willing." So it was with me. The meetings were the only place where there was any relief to be found from the chaotic condition of my life.

Everyone was angry, and I do mean everyone. Myself included. At this point, you couldn't make me angry. I woke up that way. All I needed was something to direct it at and anything you might say could trigger an explosion.

I talked my financial situation over with Hank Hall, one of the business friends who had helped me with cash infusions when needed. He not only recommended that I file for bankruptcy, but let me have me $6,000 for a good bankruptcy lawyer as well. This was especially generous of him since he knew he would be on the list of people that wouldn't receive the money that I owed them.

Brenda and I both met with the lawyer and it was determined that we would file separate petitions. Hers would be a Chapter 7 (straight bankruptcy) mine a Chapter 11 (a reorganization).

Everyone was doing the best he could with what he had to work with. Unfortunately, in my case what I had to work with didn't amount to much. However, to my growing amazement, *I wasn't drinking!*

After a meeting one Tuesday evening, Pat Harrison, an AA member who had been my counselor at the treatment center, invited me to go over to Greenville the next day for an AA meeting and lunch. There was someone he wanted me to meet.

"He lives way down east in Belhaven," he said. "He needs somebody to talk to."

∞∞∞∞∞

We met Nick Charles at Christine's, an upscale restaurant in Greenville. Pat and I had gone to a meeting at the High Noon Group which met in an upper room at one of the downtown churches. Nick hadn't been at the meeting.

Here was yet another great big man. About six-six and two hundred and sixty pounds, with brown eyes and graying hair. He was quiet and self-contained. He and Pat talked about food and it became apparent to me that the reason that we'd met at this restaurant was that Nick wouldn't eat just any old food. It needed to be good food that was prepared well. The food at Christine's was "edible".

I listened more than talked, and the conversation eventually worked its way around to AA and recovery. The discussion went back and forth for a few minutes in friendly debate on "the spiritual model of recovery". Finally Nick, who was obviously some form of agnostic,

119

said, "The Big Book[5] needs to be updated to reflect modern theories of time and space."

This statement got my full attention. Bill Wilson, the book's primary author, had written that it was being revealed that, "...as mankind studies the material world, outward appearances are not inward reality at all." To illustrate his point, he used the example of a "prosaic steel girder" which he said was simply, "...a mass of electrons whirling around each other at incredible speed. These tiny bodies are governed by precise laws, and these hold true throughout the material world."

I could easily agree with Bill that "real estate" is not in fact "real", but could not agree with his position on "precise laws".

The 1927 Copenhagen Interpretation of Quantum Mechanics had taught me that while probabilities could be determined with great precision, *nothing could be known for sure about an individual case.* This principal had a huge spiritual significance for me. I began talking with Nick. Thus began a great friendship.

∞∞∞∞∞∞

I was going to meetings, I got a sponsor, and I was working the steps. I was also meeting the most amazing people: George Smith, a Duplin County farm boy. Eddie-Rock Denton, a house painter and his business partner Willard Green, who quoted Plato in AA meetings.

My sponsor, Ed, was a retired Yankee commercial florist. He was also Catholic. There were very few Catholics in Eastern North Carolina at that time (there still aren't many, but more than in the '90s). They were viewed with great suspicion, as something other than "Christian".

---

[5] The term "Big Book" refers to the book *Alcoholics Anonymous,* the basic text of the AA program.

The office was a madhouse. There was trouble everywhere I looked. I was working on research projects and the bankruptcy at the same time. I used deposits on new jobs to pay the salaries and expenses of work-in-progress. Creditors were after me day and night.

A man from one of the banks asked, "Can you borrow money from your friends and family and pay us?"

"Can you lend me some money so that I can pay my friends and family?" I asked him back.

Thanksgiving rolled around and my in-laws were coming for supper. I left the office early and was in the kitchen working on shrimp and grits for the main course. Brenda was in a foul mood.

My brother Ernest had agreed to buy a mid-sized Pontiac for my family to use for transportation during the bankruptcy, since all of our cars were going to be repossessed and I would not be able to have a car in my own name for quite a while.

My wife, who had been sweeping off the porch in preparation for company, stormed into the kitchen. "I want a car in my name!" she yelled.

Being nine months sober, and a poster-child for AA, I remained perfectly calm. "Well then honey," I said. "Why don't you get a car in your name?" Being very pleased with my equanimity, I started across the kitchen to put something into the recycling bin.

"The only reason that you spend so much time at the office is so you won't have to help me around here!" she stormed.

I have no clear memory of what happened next. I had her by the throat and was bashing her head into the refrigerator. I couldn't see, I couldn't hear, I couldn't think, I couldn't breathe. I was putting every ounce of my strength into trying to break her neck.

I then found myself on the floor. I think I must have passed out from lack of oxygen.

I crawled out the back door and stumbled over to the bunk house in Mother's backyard across the street. I stretched out on a lower bunk and went to sleep.

I woke up a couple of hours later. It was dark. I went back to the house, which was now full of people. As I walked in through the front door, I saw my in-laws and some neighbors in the living room.

I kept right on walking without saying a word. Going upstairs, I stretched out on our bed, completely exhausted. Less than ten minutes later there was a knock at the door.

"Tarboro Police," a voice said.

I opened the door to find two uniformed policemen looking at me.

"Your wife has gotten an order ex-parte," the man in front said, "That means that you have to vacate these premises and that you cannot come within three hundred feet of her."

I just stared at him not knowing what to say.

"You have fifteen minutes to pack," the cop went on.

"I'll need more time than that," I told him.

"Fifteen minutes," the cop repeated.

Not knowing what else to do, I went to the closet and got my big suitcase. Putting it on the bed, I started packing. I put in underwear first, then, opening the sock drawer, started packing my handguns. The forty-four, the thirty-eight and the twenty-two.

"Hold it right there!" snapped one of the cops.

"Give those to us," said the other.

"They belong to me," I said grimly.

"You can get them back later then," one of them said. I handed the guns over and finished packing.

As we started through the bedroom door, one of the cops said, "Your wife gets the BMW." I didn't know what that had to do with anything, so I just kept walking. As we were going down the stairs, the cop said again, "Your wife gets the BMW."

Downstairs, we walked down the hall toward the front door. Passing the living room, I saw the assembly that I had passed coming in. I hadn't seen Brenda at all.

It had started raining. As I went out the door I picked up my umbrella. Outside, as we were passing my car, the same cop said for the third time, "Your wife gets the BMW."

I reacted without thinking. Using the metal tip of the umbrella, I started gouging the hood of the car. Both cops were on me in a flash. They pinned my arms behind me and handcuffed me. They then took me to their patrol car and, putting my head down, got me into the backseat. I had to sit forward because of the cuffs. There was a wire grill that separated the rear seat from the front. There were no inside door handles. *Just like in the movies,* I thought.

They took me to the magistrate's office, which was a low brick building at the rear of the county courthouse. Phil Pollock, the magistrate, was waiting for us inside. Phil was an old friend.

"Call a lawyer," he said. The cops took the handcuffs off and I called my friend Clarence Easley at home. Then we sat and waited.

Clarence came and I was released on my own recognizance after the judge cautioned me again not to come within three hundred feet of Brenda.

Not knowing where else to go, I went to Mother's. When I explained to Mother what had happened, she looked at me as if I had two heads, but said nothing.

I went upstairs to my old room, undressed and went to bed. I fell asleep eventually.

The next day, I had a meeting with my sponsor Ed and Pat Harrison. There were no more excuses. I had come to AA because I couldn't stand the idea of being a drunken, wife-beating asshole, and had managed to become a sober, wife-beating asshole. There was something that I wasn't understanding.

The next day I drove down to Belhaven for a visit with Nick. We spent the day in his kitchen, talking and making Maryland crabcakes.

After dinner, we watched Scorsese's *The Last Temptation of Christ*, which Nick managed to snag off a West Coast satellite.

The next morning I drove back to Tarboro a changed man.

∞∞∞∞∞∞

What is it that decides how things happen? What is it that decides the course our lives take? What decides what things mean?

Alexander Solzhenitsyn wrote, "The line separating good and evil passes not through states, nor between classes, nor between political parties either – but right through the human heart."

This is true. But what is it that decides which way it will go? What is it?

Doug House, an Indian medicine man that I met in AA, once gave me a translation of the word "manna". Manna was the powerful spiritual food that the Children of Israel received from God each morning to sustain them on their forty-year journey through the desert. It was the thing that kept them going.

Doug is an actual shaman, not just someone who has studied shamanism. A member of the Bear Clan, of the Oneida Indian tribe of Wisconsin, he is the real thing. He even has schizophrenia.

"Do you know what the word 'manna' actually means?" he asked me.

"No idea," I told him.

He smiled and said, "What is it?"

Chapter 11

The Aviator

January 1993

Question: How much money does it take to
fly an airplane?
Answer: All of it.

Anonymous

I didn't feel good. I didn't feel good about myself, and I didn't feel good about the world. I talked to the preacher at the Presbyterian Church.

"You were provoked," he said, when I told him what I had done to Brenda. That didn't help.

I was immersed in AA, which is said to be, "A simple kit of spiritual tools." Since these tools were at hand, I used them. I can see now that I was once again being forced to do something. I was motivated by shame, fear, guilt and remorse. I couldn't stay where I was, and for some reason I couldn't go back to alcohol. I had to move forward. This feeling bad was good.

Step Four of the AA program directed me to, "Make a searching and fearless moral inventory of myself." This was something completely foreign to me. The church's corporate confession, which amounts to, "I'm mean and bad and I eat worms, please forgive me," doesn't even come close to it.

Taking this step signaled the opening of a much more meaningful dimension of my spiritual life. In the past, I had made professions of faith several times. I had also, "Made a decision to turn my will and my life over to the care of God" (AA's 3rd Step), but the 4th Step was the beginning of my actually finding a way to go about doing that.

I talked with my sponsor Ed who really wasn't much help. This is not a criticism of Ed. There were things he simply didn't know and, as Bill Wilson wrote, "Obviously you can't transmit what you don't have." (Rasputin told his disciples the same thing.)

I read the Big Book and other AA literature, but still couldn't get a toehold. Finally, I just got a yellow legal pad and started writing down all the things that I could remember doing that I was ashamed of, beginning with my earliest memories. This turned out to be a very good thing. As a later sponsor would tell me, "There is no wrong way to get better."

I took the completed list to Ed and we did a Fifth Step: "Admitted to God, to ourselves, and to another human being the exact nature of our wrongs."

We talked it over, and I came away changed for the better. In the Gnostic *Gospel of Thomas*, Jesus said, "If you bring forth what is inside you, what you bring forth will save you. If you don't bring forth what is inside you, what you don't bring forth will destroy you." I was finding this to be true.

The 12-Step recovery program is alchemical in nature. The alchemists made gold from base metal. In my case, a wonderful new creature was being made out of a horrible, wife-beating monster.

∞∞∞∞∞

In spite of the chaos, business was good. There wasn't enough cash, but Bob Schultz's business had revived, medical research projects came, and Ben Gold's business was prospering.

I was having a fascinating time in AA with people coming and going, getting sober and drinking, living and dying. I had started meeting Nick in Greenville as often as we could both arrange it. We'd go to the High Noon Group's AA meeting, then have lunch at A Matter of Taste, one of Greenville's "fine dining" places.

Nick was talking one day about Ocracoke Cable, one of his several high-tech businesses. He'd gone out to Ocracoke Island, NC and literally built Ocracoke Cable Television with a tool box and a bucket truck. He was very proud of his work.

The Company rented a small cabin year-round that was used by work crews for the Company and by Nick's family for trips to the pristine beach.

Ocracoke is another of North Carolina's "real" islands. There is no bridge, and Nick's normal commute to work on the Island was a three-hour-and-forty-minute ferry ride across the Pamlico Sound.

"I'm going to take flying lessons," Nick said. "That way, I can go over to the Island, take care of business and come back in one day. They give lessons at the Washington (NC) airport. Come do that with me."

I wasn't interested, having made one excursion in a little Cessna some years back with my cousin Jack and finding it terrifying.

"Come on," Nick coaxed. "It'll give us something to do together."

So I agreed.

The Washington Airport turned out to be a WWII era airfield which I was to learn was a good thing. Built at a high tide of nationalism, it was a very well built facility with three nice, long runways that enabled operations under varying weather conditions.

The ground-school portion of the training was conducted in the evening, which I appreciated since it didn't interfere with business. I learned more about the weather than I had ever imagined I wanted to know, and I got a refresher course in aerodynamics. I did well in school.

Actual flight training was done in a Cessna 150, which is a very small two-seater aircraft. Watching Nick get into that little thing was rather like watching an elephant get into a Volkswagen.

My instructor was a cocky young guy of Italian descent named Jim. He wore Ray-Ban shades and looked exactly like what he was. A cocky young flying instructor.

I studied the plane's instruments and controls in the classroom, then Jim took me out to the plane.

We sat in the cockpit with me in the pilot's seat. I felt the controls and looked at the instruments. It was wonderful.

I started the engine and taxied to the runway.

On the ground, a plane is steered by pressing the right and left rudder pedals with the feet. The throttle is on the dashboard. It was an awkward and very foreign way of going, but thrilling.

After I managed to get lined up at the end of the runway, Jim showed me a blue line on the airspeed indicator that was the plane's rotation speed. The speed that I needed to reach in order to take off.

He then reached over and pushed the throttle to the firewall. The little plane began to roll, picking up speed and wandering from one side of the runway to the other due to my awkward steering.

Jim appeared disinterested.

When the airspeed needle passed the blue line, I eased back on the yoke and flew.

Years before, I had run away from a private boarding school in Virginia. My parents had sent me there in order to get me away from a girl. When they caught up with me, my parents sent me to a psychologist who lived and practiced in a suburb of Washington, DC. They did this in a futile attempt to get some understanding of what was going on with me.

I lived in the doctor's home with him and his wife for a week, during which time I had many therapy sessions, and was tested extensively. At the end of my treatment, the doctor gave my father his report, and a healthy bill.

My parents wouldn't share the doctor's findings with me in detail, but they did tell me that his assessment was that I'd make a good race-car driver or pilot, but not a very good florist. He was right.

We stayed in the airport's traffic pattern that morning doing touch-and-go landings. Jim had to help with the landings that day, but I was fully committed to the undertaking.

∞∞∞∞∞

July was coming, and with it the North Carolina State AA Convention. This year the Convention, which was expecting about 2,500 attendees, was to be held in Charlotte. I planned to go.

A big part of my wanting to go to the Convention was a hope that I might connect with a girl that I'd met at another AA Convention that had been held in Black Mountain, NC a month or so before.

After a meeting of the Noon Group in Greenville, a friend, Cathy Spain, said that she'd be at the Convention too and would be meeting an old friend of hers who would be driving up from Spartanburg, South Carolina.

I got to the Convention feeling down in the dumps. The hotel was full of cigarette smoke. People were drinking coffee and having a good time. I didn't see the girl that I'd hoped to connect with in the crowd, but I did run into Cathy and her friend. Once that happened, the girl that I'd hoped would be there didn't matter anymore.

I went up to my room and got cleaned up and stretched out on the bed for a few minutes. Giving up on a nap, I went back downstairs. I found her at once in the crowd. She stood looking at me from across the room, shifting her weight from one foot to the other like a little girl in a schoolyard.

Anne Bunting was a beauty. Not the kind of fashion model beauty that Brenda was, but an aristocratic beauty that reeked of intelligence and education.

She was originally from Robersonville, a small town located a few miles east of Tarboro, and she was an enthusiastic lover of that part of the world. Anne had grown up, literally, on the same highway that ran past my family's front door.

She had gone to the University at Chapel Hill at a time when few women had gone there, married an Eastern North Carolina boy that was a distant cousin of mine, and ended up in Spartanburg when her husband's work took him there.

She was a professional stockbroker and had been sober for nine years.

We talked for hours, not noticing the Convention going on around us. There was a powerful attraction. I couldn't bring myself to suggest going back to my hotel room, so the weekend ended with my driving back to Tarboro completely distracted and obsessed by her.

∞∞∞∞∞

An alcoholic Lutheran minister once told me, "There is no happily ever after in life. Life comes in episodes – like Batman."

This episode in my life would be engendered by the constellation, or coming together, of four disparate phenomena: a woman (*always* an ingredient in any of my episodes), an airplane, a new business partner, and a psychologist.

A Buddhist might see this constellation through the lens of the Doctrine of Mutual Arising, which looks for things that "like to happen at the same time".

A Jungian would probably say that these acausal coincidences were examples of synchronicity.

Whatever language one uses, powerful changes were underway in my life.

The drive from Tarboro to Spartanburg was five-and-a-half hours, which was too much for me. *However, I had already started working on a pilot's license before I met Anne.*

The cost of flying is exorbitant, even if one is deducting every last nickel of it as a business expense. *However, my already existing relationship with Hank Hall would evolve into a full-blown business partnership which would put an end to my cash crisis.*

The new relationship would be painfully transforming for both Anne and me. *However, she was already in therapy with a Jungian-type analyst before she met me.*

In a sense, all the ingredients for my transformation were already there. They just had to constellate.

∞∞∞∞∞∞

I went home and wrote a note to Anne about the beauty of our meeting and the chemistry that had started between us. Two days later, I got a beautiful note from her, which must have been mailed the same day as I mailed mine, saying much the same thing, but in more poetic language. In the note she spoke about the "unfolding" of our relationship, and said, "As a witch, I'm fully aware of where this can lead."

A witch? I was a small town Presbyterian boy. I knew nothing about witches, except what I'd heard in church or read in books. At that point in my life, I couldn't even ask: "WWJCD?" (What would Joseph Campbell do?)

That didn't matter. I was in the grip of the Goddess, and I was going to find out what it was all about in person. I really could not do otherwise. I picked up the phone and called her. The following weekend I was on the road again.

She greeted me at her home with a foot massage. "That's Biblical!" Constance would tell me later. She was right. I began another long-distance relationship, and accelerated my flight training at the same time.

Anne had been Phi Beta Kappa at Carolina, which gave our conversations an entirely different tone than those that I'd had with Brenda.

We went to the theater. We went to the ballet. We watched Fellini movies, went to AA, and made love.

Anne took me to the Unitarian Church, where I met a "real live Pagan" and a Jewish Sunday school teacher.

∞∞∞∞∞∞

Back in North Carolina, my flying instructor taught me that, "You land an airplane by making a series of small corrections." After that I soloed, which was quite a thrill, and I was ready for my Long Cross-Country training flight.

On the Long Cross-Country, I would be on my own in the little Cessna. My assignment was to fly from the Washington Airport, southeast to the little town of Southport. There I had to buy fuel for the plane and get an official at the airport to sign my flight log. I was then to proceed northwest to the town of Southern Pines, refuel again and get another signature, then fly back to Washington.

On the day of the flight, I was so nervous that I stopped by my lawyer's office on my way out of town and made a change to my will. Just in case I didn't make it.

The trip was the most amazing experience that I'd had since losing my virginity.

The C-150 is not a powerful aircraft. It flies "low and slow". In fact, if there's a strong headwind you might look down and find yourself being passed by cars driving along an Interstate Highway.

That day though, I found myself cruising along at 3,500 feet in glorious solitude amidst a layer of puffy white clouds, as my beautiful homeland rolled beneath me. I crossed the mighty Cape Fear River and approached the coast with the ocean beyond. I made a swing out over the Atlantic and landed at the little airstrip at Southport.

Donald Trump on his best day could not have felt more powerful than I did as I strode across the airport's apron to order fourteen gallons of aviation fuel from the attendant.

∞∞∞∞∞

In Tarboro, my list of "go-to" places for money had dried up. As a result of my felonious behavior, no bank in town would let me have even a checking account, much less a loan. The bankruptcy lawyer had made a call, and a small bank in Greenville allowed me to have a basic business checking account.

The friends that would help me meet payrolls were down to two. One of these was Hank Hall. Finally one day he said to me, "Adam, if I'm going to keep doing this, I'm going to need to *own* part of your business.

"There really couldn't be a worse time for me to do this," he went on. "All of my lines of credit are tied up in the warehouse business. All I've got left to work with is ten, no fifteen thousand dollars a month in uncommitted cash. If you can work with me that way, then we can do something."

I felt like the heavens had opened up and rained money on me, and agreed at once. We settled the details of the plan, then Hank had his lawyer draw up incorporation papers for a new company. 21st Century Copernicus, Inc.

The "Copernicus" part of the name had come from Nick Charles. Nick had called the office one day and gotten my answering machine.

Annoyed at being invited to "leave a detailed message", he'd left an explanation of Copernicus' theory of the heliocentric universe.

When I heard this message, it occurred to me that there was a philosophical parallel between Copernicus' macrocosmic revelation and my work on my own microcosmic egocentricity. I had adopted Copernicus, Inc. as my business identity.

Hank had supplied the "21st Century" part of the name pointing out that we were fast approaching the new millennium and needed to affirm that we planned on being a part of it.

This new arrangement had the effect of freeing up all the time and energy that I'd been spending chasing money and talking to creditors, and allowed it to be used for developing new business.

∞∞∞∞∞

In Spartanburg, I was moving toward a third marriage. We had an incredible amount of common ground in our backgrounds and a shared interest in the arts. Our immersion in and devotion to the process of recovery seemed to make a life together a perfect idea.

I was spending as much time as I could in South Carolina. I would leave Tarboro on Thursday morning and return on Monday afternoon. Constance did a beautiful job of managing the office and I found it easy to work from Anne's den. All I needed was a telephone and a computer. The company was expanding more into the medical research field, and business was brisk.

One night after an AA meeting, Anne confronted me. "Why were you looking so long at that blond woman?" she asked.

I didn't know what she was talking about and told her so.

"I know that you're going to look at other women, but it really hurts me when you look too long," she persisted.

I was gripped by a knot of fear. Averting my eyes, I said, "Honey, I would never intentionally do anything to hurt you. I hope you know that. I'll try to be more mindful." We got in the car and drove home.

I honestly didn't know what she was talking about, but hadn't been able to look her in the eye and tell her so. This insecurity on both our parts was a worm that would ultimately devour the relationship.

∞∞∞∞∞

I made an appointment with the FAA examiner in Goldsboro. My instructor signed my log, authorizing me to make the short hop by myself, and I went to be examined for a pilot's license.

Mr. Moneypenny (no relation to James Bond's girlfriend) was ready for me when I arrived. I took the written part of the exam, which was no problem, then we went out to the plane.

After directing me to an altitude of 1,500 feet, the examiner put me through a series of maneuvers, sitting in stoic silence while I demonstrated my competence. He had me do a stall, which meant that I gave the plane full throttle and pointed it straight up until it lost speed, stopped flying, and fell. I did a textbook recovery, and we flew on.

Moneypenny then reached over and pulled the throttle to idle, taking away my engine. This simulated emergency was intended to have me demonstrate that I could locate a suitable area to put the disabled plane down safely by gliding it in.

If you're going to have this kind of emergency, Eastern North Carolina is a perfect place to do it. It's as flat as a pool table, with plenty of open fields. You really should be able to handle it.

But I couldn't.

Back at the airport, Moneypenny gave me a pink slip, indicating that I'd failed the exam. "You're going to be fine," he said kindly. "The rest of your maneuvers were perfect. Go home and practice, then come back to me. You won't have to take the whole exam over, just the last part.

"I've been doing this a long time, and when you do get your license, I think you'll find that you are the best "engine out" pilot that you know."

This proved to be the case. I was to have three actual "engine out" situations in single-engine aircraft in my flying career and handled them all beautifully.

I was back in Goldsboro in two weeks and passed the test. "Well," said Moneypenny, "You are one."

"What?" I smiled.

"A pilot," he smiled back as he gave me my license. "Now what this really is, is a license to *learn* to fly. Be careful. Watch out for the weather; it'll kill you, and have a good time."

Two days later, I got checked out to fly a Cessna 172. The 172, or Skyhawk, is the Honda Civic of airplanes. Nothing fast or fancy, just good basic transportation. It's probably the smallest airplane that's powerful enough to plan trips in.

That Thursday, I rented a Skyhawk and flew to Spartanburg. The airplane cut the travel time from five-and-a-half hours to two-and-a-half hours, and completely changed the nature of the commute. Now, instead of drudgery, the trip was a thrilling adventure.

I flew over Raleigh and looked down (literally and figuratively) on the people having to deal with the Beltline traffic below me.

Heading west at 4,500 feet, I crossed familiar ground. I could make out Greensboro in the distance to my right. Soon I could make out the Charlotte skyline ahead, and ATC (Air Traffic Control) vectored me through their busy airspace and directly over the city.

I landed at the Spartanburg Downtown Airport, which is about a mile from Anne's house, in a light rain. This was the first of about a thousand aeronautical adventures that I would be privileged to have.

Adventures that would change the way that I thought about the world and my place in it.

∞∞∞∞∞

In a year, Anne and I were married in a private ceremony in her living room. The simple ceremony was performed by a Unitarian minister, with Anne's three daughters as the only attendants.

There were many happy times and a great deal of personal growth for both of us. However, the worm of insecurity around the "looking too long" at other women was at work.

Anne would confront me and I would tell her that I didn't know what she was talking about. As the number of these incidents grew, I became more and more fearful, and tried harder and harder to "get it right". As was the case with Catherine Gibson, the harder I tried, the worse things got. When she asked me to join her in therapy sessions with an analyst that she'd been seeing for a number of years, I agreed at once. Both of us needed some relief.

One of my great spiritual teachers, Sam Roundtree, has often told me that, "There is no greater than, or less than." By this he meant that we are all equal in the sight of God. However, some people I have met have provided me with so many lessons that they have shaped huge parts of who I have become. Our therapist, Robert Heatherly, was to be one of those.

The night after our first session, I had the following, very powerful dream:

> In the dream, I was with Eddie Patterson and Ty Hall. They were my boyhood friends, but in this dream they were older. They had aged along with me.
>
> I had a very wonderful, powerful, fully-equipped, red Ford Mustang, and took my friends for a ride.

Eddie really admired the car, and said that he would be getting one like it.

Ty stopped him and told him that he would not be doing that. He told him that this was <u>my</u> car, and that it was in <u>my</u> name.

Then I woke up.

I remembered the dream about cars that I'd had years before at the time that my father was throwing me out of his house. I also remembered Brenda's ranting about wanting a car in her own name.

I didn't fully understand the meaning of either of these dreams, but the second one seemed to be telling me that I had indeed found my own car. A car that was in my name. A way of going that was my own.

∞∞∞∞∞

Some of the people at the Washington Airport where I was renting the Skyhawks got together and made me an offer.

Since I was doing a lot of flying now, they said that they would find an especially nice plane, buy it, and then lease it to me. This arrangement would allow me to fly more for less money, and would let me keep the plane at the Tarboro Airport which was a mile-and-a-half from the office, rather than driving to Washington every time I wanted to go somewhere.

I talked it over with my partner Hank, who agreed that it was a good idea. "If you're going to be flying that much though, I want you to go ahead and get an instrument rating," he added.

My basic private pilot's license allowed me to fly wherever I needed to go, but I was not trained or authorized to fly through clouds. My instructor had taken me into a cloud once to show me what it was like, and that one experience was enough to convince me not to do it.

It was like someone had thrown a blanket over us. I became immediately disoriented, and Jim had had to come to my rescue at once. I would need to receive considerable additional training, before the "rating" could be added to my license.

I agreed to lease the plane and made arrangements for the instrument training at the Spartanburg Airport.

The guys in Washington found the perfect airplane for me. The late-model blue and white Skyhawk was well equipped for instrument flying, and had other extras such as long-range fuel tanks. It was gorgeous. I happily signed the lease and flew the plane back to Tarboro.

Corporate aviation, even at this basic entry level, is a powerful business tool. Now, when I left Tarboro for Spartanburg on Thursday morning, I could swing by Winston-Salem enroute and have a visit, and perhaps lunch, with Ernest and his colleagues at the medical school, building relationships there.

On Monday mornings, before heading for Tarboro, I could first fly west to Atlanta for meetings with pharmaceutical or academic clients. Leaving Atlanta, I would then get the little Cessna up to 7,500 feet, catch a nice tailwind, and sail all the way to the little airport in Tarboro nonstop.

For fun, I could take Anne on daytrips to Charleston, or weekend excursions to Amelia Island, Florida (the first island on Florida's East Coast). On one of these trips, we continued south to Fort Lauderdale after our weekend at the beach for a visit with Bob Schultz and his wife Gloria.

Bob had moved from Asheville to Seattle five years earlier to be closer to his family. Our business relationship had continued, but I hadn't had any personal contact with him in that time. Now Bob and Gloria were vacationing in South Florida which made him more reachable.

Anne and I waited for him at the airport. After his flight landed, Bob walked through the airport lobby, passing right in front of me without recognizing me. I had to call him back.

When I asked him why he hadn't known me, he replied, "You no longer look like the debauched scion of an old Southern family."

∞∞∞∞∞

The little airplane was a joy. The training for the instrument rating, however, was intense. It was actually much more difficult than the work for the original license.

My teacher was a sixty-year-old woman with many years of experience. Everyone where she worked called her "Mama". I called her Mrs. Orr.

Mrs. Orr would have me taxi to a takeoff position on the runway, then put on a pair of foggles. Foggles are glasses that prevent you from seeing where you are going. The top portion of the lenses are opaque. There is a narrow transparent section that allows the wearer to see the airplane's instrument panel. I had to learn to take off and fly using only the plane's instruments, with no visual input at all.

This kind of flying is extremely counter-intuitive. You have to abandon the senses that have guided you through life and rely on a completely different set of inputs. If you fail to do this, and go back to using your senses, you will end up like John F. Kennedy, Jr. (a pilot who wasn't instrument rated): dead.

For landings, you approach the airport using instruments. Then you descend into the unknown using electronic signals from below to a point where either you see the runway and land the plane, or abort the landing, go back up, and try something else. Before my training was done, Mrs. Orr told me that I made the best landings "coming from under the hood" that she'd ever seen. I have never received an accolade that pleased me more.

No sooner had I gotten my rating than I needed to fly to Columbia Missouri to finalize a contract for a research project.

The weather on the morning of my departure was abysmal. The airport was "socked in". The weather was "below minimums", and no one was flying. Conventional wisdom (an oxymoron if ever there was one) tells you never to take off under these conditions, because if something happens you'll be unable to find a place to land.

I filed my first real IFR (Instrument Flight Rules) flight plan and taxied to the end of the runway. The far end of the runway was shrouded in fog. I pushed the throttle to the firewall and took off.

As soon as my wheels left the ground I was on instruments.

I have never been more terrified. I made a turn to the west and checked in with Air Traffic Control. Following their directions, I started to climb to my cruising altitude.

I quickly realized that I was holding my breath. I wasn't breathing. I knew that if I didn't do something to deal with the terror, I was going to screw the airplane into the ground and die.

I began to sing. Somehow I knew that I'd have to breathe in order to sing. I sang the "tail number" of my plane. "I'm three-four-five-seven echo" to the tune of "I've been working on the railroad".

Soon I was much better, but I sang most of the way from Spartanburg, South Carolina to Bowling Green, Kentucky. There I made an instrument approach, refueled, and continued on to Columbia.

The meeting in Columbia was successful. On my way back to Tarboro, I stopped in Saint Louis and made a sales call at Saint Louis University. That turned out to be successful too.

Time and experience would make instrument airplane flying one of my closest friends.

∞∞∞∞∞∞

My situation at home worsened. Anne and I could scarcely go anywhere together now. Whenever we walked into a room, I would be terrified that there would be a beautiful woman there. If there was, and I saw her, and was seen seeing her, there would be yet another incident. Life together was intolerable for both my wife and me. We were both well along on the road to madness.

Dr. Heatherly suggested a couple's workshop being held in Asheville. The weekend course was entitled "Getting the Love You Want." We went, and it was an absolute disaster. It was held in a hotel that was filled with attractive women.

We drove home from Asheville without either of us speaking a word. After pulling the car under the carport in Spartanburg, I stepped out of the car, opened the lid of the trash container which was right in front of me, and slam-dunked the course material before walking into the house.

In the midst of all this pain, however, something of the greatest importance had happened. I had seen something that would change my life, and I knew it.

For one of the exercises at the workshop, we'd been given a blank sheet of paper. We'd been instructed to draw two t-graphs on the paper, one for each of our parents. We'd then been told to list the negative characteristics on the left side of their graph and their positive characteristics on the right. Try as I might, I couldn't write down a single negative characteristic for either one of my parents.

I knew at once that there was something badly wrong with this. I didn't know what was wrong, but I knew it was there, and I knew it must be very important.

It would take many sessions with Dr. Heatherly, and a lot of work on my part, to understand this misperception and to deal with it. When I had done this, however, I could extrapolate this insight into every area of my life. I would also be able to see and understand one of the basic religious problems of Western Man.

∞∞∞∞∞

With both Anne and me doing everything in our power to hold things together, our marriage fell apart. After a Unitarian Church retreat in the mountains of Virginia, we separated. We made several attempts at reconciliation, but things were hopeless.

In absolute agony, I loaded my things in the plane and flew back to Tarboro. Before leaving town though, I made my next appointment with Dr. Heatherly.

Chapter 12

The Monk
July 1998

*What is done out of love always takes place
beyond good and evil.*
- Friedrich Nietzsche

In 1957 Carl Jung wrote:

> The years, of which I have spoken to you, when I
> pursued the inner images, were the most important
> time in my life. Everything else is to be derived from
> this. It began at that time, and the later details hardly
> matter anymore. My entire life consisted in elaborating
> what had burst forth from the unconscious and
> flooded me like an enigmatic stream and threatened to
> break me. That was the stuff and material for more
> than only one life. Everything later was merely the
> outer classification, the scientific elaboration, and the
> integration into life. But the numinous beginning was
> then.

I have no way of knowing what part of Jung's direct encounter
with the unconscious was voluntary, but I know that no part of what I
was to experience was my idea.

I can also appreciate that while my experience occurred at the
time of my separation from Anne, Jung's occurred at the time of his
separation from Freud.

My dreams were filled with images of hurricanes. Often, I would
find myself at the beach cottage where I grew up. The storms would
rage and beat against the house, which would shudder under the

impact of the waves. Sometimes the waves would break in and wash through the structure.

All of this was archetypal material. I concluded that I was having the same experience as the Biblical Job had when he was confronting the whirlwind. I was directly confronting the Seven Eyes (or Spirits) of God that are mentioned in the Revelation of John.

I was living in a one-bedroom apartment on Saint Patrick Street in Tarboro. The apartment was in an early 20th century house that had been divided into four residences.

When the process began, I was unable to function. I would wake up in the morning, work with my dreams, and then have my devotional time. After that, I would go outside and walk the half-mile to the Tar River. I'd look at the river, take a leak, and walk back to the house. There, I'd curl up in a ball and go back to sleep. After a while I'd wake up and repeat the process.

The pain was incredible. Sometimes I'd be unable to see anything but white. Like a bedsheet was stretched in front of me.

I don't know how long this level of pain persisted, but eventually I recovered enough to be able to get to the office a little bit and to get to AA. However, like Jung's experience, what I was undergoing would continue for several years.

Also like Jung, I would come to count this as the most important time in my life. It was certainly enough material for more than one lifetime, and it definitely threatened to break me.

At one point, I asked Dr. Heatherly if he thought I was suicidal. "Yes," he replied. "I think you are. Do you want to take something for it?"

"No," I assured him. By then I'd gotten the idea firmly in my mind that what was happening to me was a blessing. Like my alcoholism, it would take me exactly where I needed to go.

∞∞∞∞∞

One day an AA friend, George Smith, told me that Sam Roundtree was in town. Sam was staying with one of the other members of the group and was coming to George's apartment that evening to talk.

I had seen Sam in passing at meetings, and I knew that he was something of a "famous drunk". Someone well known in the recovery community. I had come to enjoy George's company and decided to go meet this celebrity.

At George's, the room was blue with cigarette smoke. I hadn't smoked since my early 20s, and tobacco smoke was definitely a problem for me, but I waded in.

Sam is a small, wiry man. He was then about 60 years old, and habitually dressed in black from head to toe. There is a mugshot of Sam that many people mistake for Charles Manson.

He was sitting in George's recliner wreathed in smoke and explaining a section of the AA Big Book to the gathering. His voice was a whiskey and cigarette soaked rasp.

He was explaining a section of the Book in which Bill Wilson (the Book's primary author) wrote that in the throes of alcoholism, the alcoholic is not able to differentiate the true from the false. To illustrate this point, Sam was using the "Denial of Peter" from the Christian Bible.

"...So Jesus said to Peter 'man, before the cock crows you're gonna deny that you even know me.' Peter said, 'No way Master would I ever do that. For I am your most devoted follower.'" Sam continued, in a stage whisper, "Because you see, he couldn't diff-e-nciate the true from the false. About that time, a bunch of Roman soldiers got in his face about it and Peter said, 'I don't even know that cocksucker!'" The gathering gave an affirming murmur.

I listened to the discussion for as long as I could stand the cigarette smoke, then stepped outside for some air. In a few minutes, Sam followed me. "How you doin?" he asked.

"Not too well," I told him. "My wife and I have separated."

"Good!" Sam rasped. "I know everybody's been saying 'bad', I just thought you'd like to hear something different." I didn't know what to say, so I just stood there. He continued, "You know, there ain't nothing out there."

I was astounded at this. "What did you say?" I asked.

"No, there ain't nothing out there. Not a goddamned thing. Never has been."

I knew very little about Sam Roundtree, but I knew enough to be pretty sure that he'd never read the Upanishads, Schopenhauer, or Plato. Nor did I imagine that he was up to speed on the metaphysics of contemporary physics. What was he talking about? How did he know that? I wrote down his phone number, told him goodnight and went back to my apartment.

∞∞∞∞∞

"When the student is ready, the teacher will appear." This tired old statement is still around because it's true. The Universe does indeed provide me with what I need; my part in the process is to accept what comes as something that I need. AA didn't really give me that principle, I had to get it from somewhere else. For me, it takes a lot of practice. I have been to about a thousand meetings on "letting go", but can't remember one on "letting come".

Wait though. There are plenty of meetings on "Acceptance". Maybe I can work "letting come" into that.

I called Sam, and he elaborated on the "Ain't nothing out there" idea. "All that's out there, is a reflection of me," he said. When I told him that was basic Hinduism, he said, "Hindu, mydo, youdo. I don't know anything about that." And he didn't!

We talked on, and he said more things that amazed me. "You're looking for an answer, but you've already got it. You were born with it."

"The reason that you feel so unique, is 'cause you are."

"The Book[6] says that either God is everything or he's nothing. Well if He's everything, that don't leave much."

"Pain is the touchstone of spiritual growth. You may not want me praying for you. I'll pray that you lose your wife, your job, your home, and end up in jail."

When I relayed all this stuff to my friend George, he put the icing on the cake. "If there is any selfishness in him, I can't find it," he said.

I got in my airplane and flew to see Sam at his home in Statesville. The houses where Sam has lived have become grander over the years, but their basic aura hasn't changed. They have all been sacred spaces. Creatures of all types are attracted to where he lives. Some are four-legged and some are two. There are many kinds of birds.

Many of the creatures are wounded. All of them come there for sanctuary.

There are also many kinds of plants and flowers. Sam once said to me, "I'd like for you to meet my spiritual advisors." He pointed to two climbing green vines that grew on either side of his front door. Exactly like the pillars of a temple. "This one is Sigmund," he said. "That one is Freud. What Sigmund don't know, Freud does."

∞∞∞∞∞∞

Now I had two primary spiritual teachers. They were from different schools, but the schools were related. Sam Roundtree was a

---

[6] Reference to the book *Alcoholics Anonymous*.

drunk. A wino who had been transformed by his disease into a fine man and a highly realized spiritual being. True man and true God.

Robert Heatherly had arrived at the same place by a much different path. He had experienced war and many other unnamed trials. He became a Christian mystic and a psychologist.

The science of psychology is a very big tent. About the same size as the "religion" tent. There are many varieties. Some have been helpful to me, others have definitely not. Robert is not a clinician. He, like Jung, is a doctor of the soul. I don't think Robert would be offended at being called a Neo-Jungian.

Alcoholics Anonymous, Sam's school, owes its very existence to Carl Jung. Jung treated a wealthy American for alcoholism and sent him home with the idea that *only a vital spiritual experience* could solve his problem. From that beginning, which was so small that it didn't even rate a mention in Jung's writing, came the spiritual model of recovery that has saved millions of men and women.

I would talk with both of these men on the phone and would make regular trips to see them in person. I'd leave Tarboro and fly to Statesville for a visit with Sam, then fly south to Spartanburg for an appointment with Robert. Then home.

Robert used depth psychology to guide me into the dark places in my psyche that held the unacknowledged parts of myself which would ultimately bring healing. This was painful and exhausting work that would often leave me feeling very vulnerable.

The work that I did with Sam was equally intense but in a different way.

I came across a review of a new airplane in one of my flying magazines. The author said, "The warranty provides a level of support that can't be found anywhere else, except in AA. And I don't mean American Airlines."

Sam held my hand and talked to me. The blinding pain was no longer an unbroken continuum, but it was still fierce, and it was still a daily companion.

"You're in the rock-crusher," Sam would tell me. "You are being made ready for something wonderful. I could tell you about it, but you wouldn't understand me. You're right on time."

I called Sam every day. Or twice-a-day, or three times. I don't see how he stood it.

He had me work on another 4th Step, this one much more analytical than the one that I had done with my sponsor Ed. We focused not on what I had done, but why I had done it. Patterns emerged, and I could see that I didn't have as many problems as I thought I had.

Everyone who goes through this process finds something different. That's what makes it so effective. You find your own way of understanding, "the exact nature of your wrongs".

Bill Wilson had written about the "basic instincts of life". The instincts for sex, security, and society. With this 4th Step, something clicked in me, and I was able to see parallels between these instincts and the Temptations of the Buddha. I could also relate them to the first three chakras of Kundalini Yoga. This realization showed me a path that I'd not seen before. I had a different way of dealing with what life brought me.

For example, if life brought me a scary situation, the real problem was not what was happening, but my *fear* of what was happening. What was happening was actually a gift. It was God's way of making a better man out of me.

Sam helped me to see that when one of these instinctive drives was out of balance, it would pull the other two out as well. There was plenty of work to do.

∞∞∞∞∞∞

My trusty Skyhawk had come to the point in its life that the engine needed to be rebuilt in order for it to be considered safe for IFR flying. The owners didn't want to spend the money to do this, so I sadly returned the plane to them and terminated the lease. This meant that I was back to flying rented aircraft, which had the effect of moving me up to flying more powerful aircraft based in nearby Greenville. These aircraft have features such as variable pitch propellers and retractable landing gear. They are stronger and faster. Since I was no longer living part-time in Spartanburg, I saw this as another fortunate coincidence.

I was in touch with a man named John Ridgeway, an AA friend from Lexington, Kentucky. Anne and I had met the Ridgeways at the International AA convention in San Diego in '95, and become fast friends.

John was (he is now dead) an authentic, conventional Christian, who lived his beliefs. I had great admiration for him.

John was a supporter of the Bagdad AA Retreat, which was held twice a year near the little town of Bagdad, Kentucky, which is located midway between Lexington and Louisville. John wanted me to come to the November retreat. I agreed to attend, and to bring my good friend George Smith and another man, Marvin Locklear, with me.

I rented a Cessna 182 for the trip. The 182 is the faster, more muscular brother of the Skyhawk. We took our time getting there, stopping for a Coke at a small airstrip in the Blue Ridge Mountains. John met us at the Lexington Airport and drove us to the retreat center, which is in a beautiful wooded area.

As always, there was coffee, cigarette smoking, and good fellowship. John was very well known in the Kentucky recovery community and got us settled comfortably in short order.

The next day, George and I went for a walk in the woods, where we ran into a couple of girls. We struck up a conversation and walked on together. Nature paired me with an attractive blond, who turned out to be a lawyer from Lexington. We talked about books, recovery, aviation, and her experience working as a lawyer.

The next day I saw her again, but she seemed strangely distant. I was definitely interested in her, but I didn't think I ought to try to chase her down.

The conference was a good one, and the trip home was a joy, with a ripping tailwind at 9,000 feet.

Two days later she called.

There is a spiritual principle, which Robert Heatherly refers to as the Imago Dei, or "Image of God". This principle says that we will attract into our lives people and circumstances that will help us to become whole. This principle is not a theory, it's a fact. I know it is, because I have experienced it. More than once. It is (as I have mentioned before) God's way of making a man out of me.

I hadn't been talking to this woman very long before I realized that this was going to be what Robert calls an Imago relationship. It was a recurrence, at a whole new level, of a difficulty that I'd had for my most of my life.

I resolved at once to take care of my unfinished business with this dynamic, so that I wouldn't have to deal with it again. I knew that the process was going to hurt like hell, and I knew that in order to heal, I was going to have to go *all the way* through it.

This woman, whom George christened, "The Lawyer Chick" had important things in common with other influential women in my life. She had been born to a very powerful woman who had been paired with a man who was seriously flawed. I can trace this structure in the families of women in my life going back to when I was fifteen years old. A bear of a mother and an absent or ineffective father.

She would come close, then pull away, disappearing for days. I knew that to pursue her wouldn't work, and that I needed to sit and wait for her to come back. Which she would eventually do. The relationship was my worst nightmare, but it was also exactly what I needed.

"When God works, everybody gets better," said Sam.

"It feels like she's taken your soul," Robert said. And it did.

"You're asking her to do something that she can't do," said John Ridgeway. "It's like asking her to walk with a broken leg." And it was.

"Why don't you leave her alone," said Robert. "She's busy trying to save her life."

"When God works, everybody gets better," said Sam.

She was a wonderful person, and I did get to spend some time with her that was very precious. She finally got the courage to move to New York City to be treated by a doctor who specializes in her disorder. I haven't seen her since, nor have I had to confront the problem that I had with my side of that equation. I don't believe that it will come back again.

∞∞∞∞∞

After my separation from Anne, and as soon as the pain had subsided enough for me to think, my reading program had really taken off. I'd always been somewhat "bookish", but that trait suddenly became much stronger.

Philosophy, psychology, mythology, poetry, and great novels. Everything I read had deep spiritual significance.

Movies too had deep meaning. *The Matrix* trilogy and Clint Eastwood's *Unforgiven* carried the weight of scripture.

I would become overloaded and try to escape into an orgy of mindless action flicks. But even there, there seemed to be profound messages. Except for Steven Seagal. He had nothing for me.

Hurricane Floyd arrived bringing a reenactment of the Biblical Deluge. There was water everywhere. There were 42 inches of it in my office. We couldn't get out of town. We lost electrical power, and the water purification system was polluted. There were rumors of piles of bodies in the immigrant communities.

I had been reared on the interpretation of the Great Flood given by the Christian Bible. By that account, God sent the flood because of His displeasure with mankind. It was a catastrophic disaster and a punishment.

In my reading though, the works of Joseph Campbell offered another interpretation. In other cultures, this event is seen as a cleansing. A kind of giant douche. A "Behold I make all things new" event.

After the waters subsided, I looked around me. The builders and remodelers were working at full capacity. The hardware and lumber companies were having record sales. Disaster recovery teams from churches near and far were in town, "on a mission from God".

Families had been uprooted and taken to new places, where one day a child would ask his grandfather, "Granddaddy, how did we come to live in Philadelphia?"

The response would be, "We came here after the Great Flood of '99."

I looked at the world around me and, "Behold, it was very good."

∞∞∞∞∞

I was going into the Post Office one day to get the mail, when I met a man coming out. "They're flying planes into the World Trade Center," he said.

"Who is?" I asked.

"I don't know, but it's awful!" he said, hurrying on his way.

I picked up the mail and went back to the office, where Constance and the rest of the workers were gathered around the television in the breakroom. CNN was playing and replaying images of the destruction. Everyone was speechless.

My mind at once went back in time to a day that I had spent on Anne's couch trying to work.

Ben Gold had called with the news that another of his clients had declared bankruptcy and we wouldn't be paid the money that they owed. This was not the first time that this had happened, but the loss was much bigger this time around. $40,000.

"Are you guys queer, or what?" yelled my partner Hank. "Sue him."

Bob Schultz told me the same thing, but in a much gentler way. "It's time for you to take back your manhood."

I was furious with Ben for putting me in this position. As I sat on the couch, an idea came into my mind. It was more than an idea, really. It was a story.

Ben Gold's office was in a gray building that overlooked the harbor of the coastal town of Beaufort, North Carolina. The plan which grabbed me was,

> *What I need to do, is take the plane to the Morehead-Beaufort*
> *Airport, top it off with gas, swing it out over the harbor, and fly*
> *it right through that cocksucker's front door.*

As I said, this was more than a passing thought. I could picture the events in my mind and it gave me pleasure. I ran the plan through my head again and again. It made me feel warm and fuzzy.

Now I was watching as my scheme was played out in horrifying detail in New York. I knew at once that the terrorist who had attacked New York and I were alike. We were the same man.

When I told people about this insight, they said, "Yeah, but you didn't actually do it." They were missing the point. Osama Bin Laden and I were brothers. Sam was right. "All that's out there is a reflection of me." There are not two kinds of people. The recipes may be different but the ingredients are the same.

...We step on the toes of our fellows and they
retaliate. Sometimes they hurt us, seemingly without
provocation, but we invariably find that at some time
in the past we made decisions based on self which later
placed us in a position to be hurt.
So wrote Bill Wilson.

America had been stepping on other people's toes for quite some
time. Sometimes with the best of intentions, but generally without
being aware of the full implications of what we were doing. *We know
not what we do.*

We would find Bin Laden and kill him. That is something that I
think had to happen. I have heard it said that death by lethal injection
is a natural death. It is the natural consequence of your actions. Bin
Laden's death was the natural consequence of his actions. That
doesn't keep it from making me very sad.

The "sad-making" part of what took place on September 11,
2001 was that we missed the lesson. Again.

We have become exporters of arms, ammunition, and military
expertise. Some of what we have been sowing came home to us. It
was the natural consequence of our actions. We will reap what we
sow. (Who said that anyway?)

America may very well continue down the road we are on. I
don't know where we're going, and I only have one vote. In my case,
it was the 4th Step that enabled me to see things differently, and I had
to be forced by circumstances to take that step. If 911 wasn't enough
for us, I wonder what will be?

∞∞∞∞∞∞

The elevation of the airport at Greenville, NC is 0. Sea level.
The rest of the community's elevation is about 50 feet above sea level,
but the airport was built in a low area. As a result, the Great Flood

wiped out most of what was there, including the rental planes that I was using.

Once again, disaster moved me to a better situation. I was nudged upward into flying a Beechcraft Duchess. The Duchess is a twin-engine airplane. Classified as a "light twin", it's one of the lightest of the light twins. Even so, it was a big move up for me. It is powered by the same engine that my old Skyhawk had, but now there were two of them. Fuel capacity and consumption increased correspondingly, but the increase in the rate of climb and cruising speed were heady stuff. It felt like I was flying a fighter plane.

After an appointment with Dr. Heatherly, I could pop over for a visit with John Ridgeway in Kentucky, then zip home in nothing flat. Sales calls in Washington DC, Atlanta, or Cincinnati were "layups". I swung by Statesville and picked up Sam and his wife Edith and took them to Florida for a few days at the beach at Amelia Island.

∞∞∞∞∞

Some friends in Chapel Hill were putting together a proposal for a huge project. The North Carolina Survey. It was to be a massive longitudinal tracking study, which would be used by officials in Raleigh to develop and evaluate economic development statewide. Once in place, it would continue indefinitely. Many people were involved in the planning. There were statisticians, demographers, and economists. Once we got involved, Hank accessed an important political connection. Then there was that element as well.

Our company's role would be to provide logistical support; data collection and management. As usual, we were to be the "low-tech" part of a "high-tech" operation, but the sheer size of this contract would make it a life-changing thing.

For all of my business life, I had been something of an "elephant hunter". I had always imagined that one day I would come across something so big that it would redefine me as a businessman. Now it was happening! I had the elephant in my sights.

I was on it full time, going to meetings, preparing budgets, and writing our part of the proposal. The closer we got, the better things looked.

One day, driving home from a particularly productive meeting in Chapel Hill, I gave Hank a call.

"We're about to change your role in the Company," I told him. "From now on, instead of putting money *in*, you're going to be taking money *out*!"

Something changed right that minute. I couldn't imagine what it was, but I felt it. From that day on, Hank became increasingly irritable and hard to get along with. I mentioned this to Sam.

"Control," said Sam. "He's losing control. You won't have to depend on him after this thing happens."

This would not have occurred to me, since all I wanted to do was to give Hank more money, but it turned out to be true.

Two weeks later, Hank came to my apartment. "You're going to sign a letter," he told me. "You're going to sign a letter stating that you will not make any purchases or enter into any contracts without the express written consent of C.H. Hall."

Here it came again. That nameless force that made key decisions for me took over. I wasn't going to sign any letter. There was no wondering about it, and no fear of what it might cost me. I refused.

For about a minute, Hank was speechless. When he recovered he said, "You don't understand! Everybody's got one of those letters. My son-in-law owns the warehouse business and he's got one of those letters."

That didn't matter. By then I'd realized that the business wasn't going to survive without Hank, but that didn't matter either. I knew right then that there was a part of me that wasn't for sale, and knowing that felt wonderful.

The dissolution happened much quicker than I could have imagined. The proposal for the North Carolina Survey wasn't funded. What had appeared to be a sure thing didn't happen. But, after what I'd found out about myself, that didn't seem to matter.

Next, in yet another acausal coincidence, we lost the data entry contract with the pharmaceutical company that had been in place for five years. Once again, this loss didn't seem like the end of the world.

I flew the Duchess to Gaithersburg, Maryland, then took the Metro into Washington for a meeting with *The Learning Channel.* A consultant from Alabama and I had made a research proposal.

We struck out.

Leaving Gaithersburg, I few east over Baltimore, then followed the coast back down to North Carolina. Ten miles from the Greenville Airport, at an altitude of 8,000 feet, I took a long last look at the view from the top of the world. Then, I pulled the throttles to idle, put the flaps down ten degrees, and started a long, slow glide to a final landing.

You land an airplane, by making a series of small corrections.

After 911, I heard a story about a man who was on the 85th floor of the World Trade Center when the attack came. Miraculously, he rode the wreckage down and ended up in the basement. Alive, but with both his legs broken.

I had a similar experience, but when the dust had settled I could still walk. I closed the door to the office, locked it, and walked away.

Chapter 13

The Thespian
March 2002

Both?... To lose one parent may be regarded as misfortune...to lose both seems like carelessness.

- Oscar Wilde

I was unemployed, and didn't have a clue about what to do with the rest of my life. I had been in business for myself for over twenty years.

My friend Nick Charles said to me, "Adam I'm afraid that you, like myself, have become basically unemployable." It had been a very long time since I'd had a boss and been in a position where I had to show up at a particular time.

When the office closed, I lost my connection to the Internet. This situation initiated my practice of going to the Public Library every day to look at my email, and to find out what was happening in the world. I am still doing this. Every day but Sunday.

Walking across the Library parking lot one morning, I saw Roberta Cashwell across the street getting her newspaper.

Roberta, a Tarboro native, had moved home after a successful career as a financier in New York. She'd hit the ground running when she got back, buying the old Marrow house on Main Street, opening a bookstore, and restarting the Tar River Players (the local amateur theater company).

We had a very pleasant conversation, and the next evening I drove out to the Community College to audition for a part in Hart &

Kaufman's *You Can't Take It With You*. This seemed particularly appropriate, given my circumstances.

The play is set in the home of a Martin Vanderhof, and recounts the adventures of a family who ignore the government and are completely unattached to money. They live in a house, "...where you do as you like, and no questions asked."

The director of the play was Jane Stanton, a New Yorker who had come down to Tarboro to play the role of a crusty old New Yorker directing a community theater group.

Jane cast me in the role of Mr. De Pinna, an eccentric friend of the family who worked in the basement of the Vanderhof home manufacturing fireworks.

Even though I'd never been in a play before, I had no problem "getting into character", since I'd been "in character" with Mr. De Pinna my whole life.

I enjoyed the camaraderie of the company, the rehearsals and the six performances. The experience of live theater appealed to me because no two performances are exactly alike.

∞∞∞∞∞∞

I called Norris Tolson, who was the political friend that Hank had introduced into the group working on the North Carolina Survey. When we'd met, we had "clicked" at once.

Norris had been born into a prominent family in nearby Pinetops. Coming home after a successful career in business, he'd gotten interested in state politics and the economic development of the State. He has held several offices in Raleigh, including Secretary of Revenue for North Carolina.

"If I were going to start a business, and needed someone to run it, you'd be the man I would call," he said. "If I couldn't get you, then the second man I'd call would be Al Delia. He's working over at ECU

(East Carolina University), running their survey research facility. Why don't you give him a call?" He gave me Al's phone number.

I had met Al some years before when we'd worked together on a political campaign for Congressman Walter B. Jones, Jr. We had helped with Walter's first campaign for the United States Congress.

Walter had run as a Democrat. When he lost the election, he felt that he'd been treated shabbily by the Democratic Party, and he became a Republican. Al and I had never been thanked for our part in that changeover, by either party.

"It's strange that you called," Al said when I got hold of him. "Your name came up just the other day."

The University's Survey Research Lab was in trouble. The woman who was in charge of the Lab had worked her way up through the ranks, and although she was a very capable person in many areas, conducting survey research wasn't one of them. The Lab had lost credibility on the campus and had disappointed enough outside clients to ruin its reputation in the business community as well. It was about to close. I met with Al and agreed to come on board on a consulting basis to see if I could turn the situation around.

Al and I were "birds of a feather". For over twenty years, my business career had been spent on the fringes of the academic community. I'd provided support services to people who were either MDs, Ph.D.s, or both.

Al was a politician and economic developer. The University had hired him to interact with other lobbyists and the elected officials in Raleigh and Washington, DC. He too lived on the fringes of the academy.

"I've always been the least educated man in the room," I told him.

"Me too," he smiled back.

The idea of my working as a consultant was his. "It will give me 'plausible deniability'," he said. "I want you to move around the campus, including and especially around the medical school, and talk to people. They have lost faith in the Lab and that's not going to be easy to rebuild. You can be a free agent, or if you prefer, a loose cannon. Just be yourself, and let's see what happens. If you step on anyone's toes, I'll just say that I didn't know what you were up to." That suited me just fine.

He gave me an office and a computer and I went to work. I liked what I was doing and enjoyed meeting University faculty from the various departments. Some of them expressed a willingness to give the Lab another chance. I was also able to bring in a couple of projects from my old client base, which changed the atmosphere from "doom and gloom" to one of hope.

My interactions with the Lab's Director were awkward to say the least, but she had no trouble seeing the handwriting on the wall and soon left for greener pastures.

Now I had a good boss, and the resources of the University to work with. Things improved rapidly at the Lab. Projects began to come in from various departments at ECU, and others from state agencies such as the Department of Transportation.

I was able to update the computers being used for interviewing and installed the latest computer-assisted interviewing software. I also had university resources at my disposal for focus group research. I'd never gotten involved with that type of research before, because of the cost and complexity of the facilities needed. Now I could.

There was a series of meetings with two members of the faculty in the School of Education, and a major project emerged. We began working on plans for a statewide study of the dynamics of what happened to students who dropped out of high school. I became completely caught up in this project, since I had dropped out of high school myself. Wondering what might have happened to me if it hadn't been for Uncle Winston's intervention filled me with energy and curiosity. It seemed to me to be a "calling", and I treated it as such.

I began pouring time and energy into meetings at various campuses of the North Carolina University system. There were video conferences and webinars, and soon I had recruited investigators at seven campuses of the University system. In addition to the faculty collaborators at ECU, there were University faculty members in Wilmington, Raleigh, Chapel Hill, Fayetteville, Pembroke, Greensboro, and Elizabeth City.

Al called me into his office one day to let me know that there was going to be a change in the management of the Lab. He had been given a promotion and would be working full time as a lobbyist for the University. He'd be spending most of his time in Washington and Raleigh, and I'd be getting a new boss. I was delighted for him and saw the move as a very positive thing for the Lab as well, since he'd be able to give ECU better access to State and Federal money that could be used for research.

Al's replacement turned out to be a sharp young Ph.D. psychologist from the East (non-medical) Campus at the University. He had been a past chair of his department, and I looked forward to working with him. The new relationship didn't work.

I didn't have the personal history with the new man that I'd had with Al, and the fact that I didn't have any sort of advanced degree would make it impossible for me to continue working as I had. While this was certainly a disappointment for me, I'd been around academics long enough not to take it personally. In that world, credentials are an absolute prerequisite for credibility. When I heard the new director tell someone that he could absolutely prove that there was no such thing as the maternal instinct, I knew I was sunk. I wouldn't be able to work with him for very long.

The steering committee for what had now been named the Dropout Study had decided to begin the project with a pilot study.

They'd asked me for a tentative budget, and I'd come up with a rough figure of $200,000.

Now with more campuses involved, and the availability of new software to facilitate analyzing larger quantities of qualitative data, I'd had to double my cost estimate for the pilot. $400,000.

The steering committee balked. At the time that I was working at ECU, they were not yet a major research university. Faculty weren't rewarded for research, they were rewarded for teaching, and they spent their time on what they were rewarded for. My brother Ernest got almost four times the funding dollars from the National Institutes of Health that year than the entire medical school at East Carolina. Committee members simply weren't used to thinking about big research dollars.

"$400,000 is really no money," I told them, but they couldn't hear me.

I made an appointment with my cousin Sam, who by this time was serving his second term in the North Carolina Senate. We met at his Tarboro office. When I explained the nature of the project, its scope, and the amount of work that had already been done, he was enthusiastic.

"North Carolina has one of the highest dropout rates in the nation," he said. "How much do you need for the pilot?"

"$400,000," I told him.

"That's really no money," he said. "Y'all go ahead. We'll get the money." I went home and slept like a baby.

When I got to work the next day the Director called me into his office and took the project away from me. He thought the budget unrealistic. I tried to explain that I had the money that we needed virtually in hand, but it did no good.

I resigned the following day, not worrying for one minute whether it was the right thing to do or not. I was getting good at leaving a job without having prospects for another one.

Once again I was rudderless. In a telephone session, Robert Heatherly suggested, "Don't just do something, sit there." So I sat. I read a lot, went to AA meetings, and continued my involvement with the Tar River Players.

I wasn't looking for work. This was intentional on my part. A teaching from my childhood came to me: "Seek ye first the Kingdom of God, and these other things will be given you as well." I took this teaching as a working hypothesis that I would test. The Rumi story about "the man who gambled himself and won" was often at the forefront of my mind. It's not that I was refusing to work, but I was resolved not to do any work that I couldn't see as having some bearing on my spiritual journey.

The Tar River Players were presenting Paul Osborn's *Mornings at Seven.* I was cast as Carl Bolton, a man who, like myself, was trying to find the meaning for his life. "Where am I in life?" he would exclaim. "I'm not where I should be at all! There is some other place where I should be!"

Unlike Carl though, I was *exactly* where I needed to be, and I knew it. I knew it not with my mind, but with my "knower", an intuitive sense that the things that were happening to me were happening for me.

Since I didn't have to worry about a job, I had plenty of time to work on the play. I was able to help Bob Kelly with the construction of the set, stage lighting and some of the other facets of live theater.

Bob was an AA friend who had retired to Tarboro after working and living for his entire life in New York City. He had worked in the production aspects of movies, theater and television. He was a prop man, and for the last five years of his career he managed that aspect of *Law and Order: Criminal Intent.* His speech and manner were rough, pretty much textbook Yankee, but he had a huge heart, and he stepped up to help me more than once when I was in need.

Mornings at Seven had a successful run and I once again found that time in the theater was time well spent.

∞∞∞∞∞∞

My son Adam had finished his work in graduate school and was preparing to leave for a tour with the Peace Corps in Ukraine. He came to stay with me at the apartment on Saint Patrick Street while he got his affairs in order for his two year adventure.

As a graduation present, I gave him my customized .44 Magnum revolver. He gave me a dreamcatcher that he had made while he was in school in the mountains of North Carolina. It was a poignant moment for me. I put the revolver up for safekeeping while he was gone and used the dreamcatcher as an icon on my little altar at the apartment.

Adam also left me his Jeep Wrangler to drive while he was gone. This was very helpful, since I'd lost my cars with the closing of the office.

I bid Adam a fond farewell and moved into a period of extreme austerity. I had no money and no job. There was food available at the homeless shelter, but my intuitive sense told me that I didn't need to do that. This was an experiment, a test of the hypothesis. I felt that to go to the food bank would mess up my variables. I didn't ask anyone for food or money for the same reason.

The experiment started working. Friends in AA would invite me for meals. Steve Franklin, the minister at the Presbyterian Church invited me for "potluck" dinners there. I was going to be ok. I didn't even lose any weight, although I once made a meal out of pecans that I had gathered on my morning walks. I ate all the food in the apartment, down to a can of chilies. Then I ate those.

"Are you physically incapable of work?" cried an exasperated Hank Hall.

"You've got to have something coming in," said the woman that I was seeing. "It's called survival!"

"Fuck survival!" I replied. And I meant it. Bill Wilson had written, "The spiritual life is not a theory. You have to live it." The time had come to "bet the farm".

A few weeks later, Steve Franklin said that he'd like for me to stop by his office. We met, and he told me that the Church had lost its sexton. He wanted to know if I'd like to fill in on a temporary basis until a replacement could be found. I could see that he was somewhat hesitant to propose this, but I was delighted! This idea made just the kind of sense that I was looking for to guide my journey.

I met with Gail Hussey, the Church Administrator, who offered me $8.75 an hour for my time. I "talked her down" to $8.00 even, because that seemed to be a "better" number, and I started work.

A side effect of my new job was that I got to spend more time with the minister. I had been going to the Tuesday morning Men's Bible Study and had come have great admiration for Steve Franklin. Now I would have opportunities to talk with him individually as well.

Steve is an authentic, believing, evangelical Christian. No longer considering myself to be a Christian, it was healthy for me to spend time with the real thing.

The action of the dialectic, that is the interaction between our opposing views, could be nothing but helpful. For both of us. Steve Franklin became my friend for life.

I was working through the process of letting go of many of the tenets of my orthodox upbringing. One of these was the Apostles Creed, which was a part of every Sunday service that I'd attended growing up. Steve told me story of his own experience at Seminary with the study of the Creed.

The faculty brought in a well-known theologian to help the prospective ministers with their consideration of the Creed. As Steve told it,

> He came to the class. When someone raised his hand with a question, he would stop him and say to the questioner "No! Just say it!" Somebody else would raise his hand with another question and he would say again, "No! Just say it!" The next question was handled in the same way, and the one after that.

The Creed was gone for me right then. I've never recited the Apostles Creed, the Nicaean Creed, or any other creed that I can think of (including the Pledge of Allegiance) since that time.

∞∞∞∞∞∞

The Tar River Players produced *Flying West* and other plays that I had no stage presence in, but enjoyed working on in a production capacity with my friend Bob Kelly.

Months passed, and my son Adam returned from Ukraine, bringing with him a beautiful fiancée.

Jolene Kellenbeck is from Montana. She is a beautiful woman of the American West, with that culture's strong individualism and sense of independence. She has made a wonderful addition to our family, and a very significant improvement in our gene pool.

Thomas Memorial hired a full-time sexton, and I was once again unemployed.

Adam reclaimed his Jeep, and I became an unemployed pedestrian. My friend Hank Hall stepped up and lent me one of his company pickups to use temporarily, but eventually he needed it back for the business.

A member of the Tarboro AA group bought a new car, and wanted to sell his old one. The "old one" was a rusty '87 Volvo station wagon that had lived most of its life on the beach at Malibu. I asked the price.

"$600," he said.

"Would $500 do?" I wondered. He agreed, and we shook hands. I didn't have $500, but told him that I'd have the money in three weeks. When I told him that, I had no idea where it would come from. Then an ex-employee showed up at the apartment and repaid a $900 loan that I'd made to her when she was working for me. I paid for the car and was rolling again.

∞∞∞∞∞

Nick Charles relapsed into drinking after ten years of sobriety. His wife Nora called me, at her wits end. "I don't know what to do!" she exclaimed. "What do you think I should do?"

"Buy him a case of wine," I replied.

"I don't have to buy him a case of wine," she responded. "We sell it at the hardware store."

She threw Nick out of the house, exiling him to the cabin on Ocracoke Island. This was very much like throwing Brer Rabbit into the briar patch, which was just what he needed. She also gave me a cell phone on their company plan so that she could stay in touch with me.

∞∞∞∞∞

The Town of Tarboro cut my lights off because I was unable to pay the bill. They stayed off for three months. I read by candlelight and cooked what meals I could scrape together on a small propane camp stove.

Eventually, the Town said that it was illegal to live without electricity, even in a house in the historic district that had been built before electric service was available. Three local churches chipped in and got me "legal" again, but I was soon evicted from the apartment because I couldn't pay my rent. Then I was unemployed *and* homeless.

An AA friend whose family was in the furniture and moving business brought a truck and moving crew to the apartment. They took my things to my old office building and stored them there.

The next morning I met the Sherriff's Deputy at the apartment. He gave me my copy of the eviction papers and I gave him the key to the apartment.

"Your cousin Jack is trying to save you," Steve Franklin told me. "He came down to the Church and wanted me to tell you to get a job flipping hamburgers or something instead of 'prancing around on stage'."

"He doesn't get it, does he?" I said to Steve.

"No, he doesn't," Steve agreed.

∞∞∞∞∞∞

Bob Kelly said that I could stay with him until things settled down. I had been on the Board of Directors of the Christian Fellowship Home in Wilson for five years at that time. When the Board met that month, I was told that the Home's Director was going to have surgery and would be out of work for six weeks.

I volunteered at once to fill in for him while he was incapacitated and the Board approved. I was to receive a small salary and a bed at the Home during this period. Once again, life provided a completely unexpected answer to the question of what to do next.

My duties at the Home were pretty simple. The Home was a halfway house for men with alcohol or drug problems. They were expected, required in fact, to go to 12-step recovery meetings, so I knew almost all of them from that venue. I screened applicants, arbitrated disputes, bought groceries, and kept records. Happy work that I enjoyed doing.

I hadn't been at it very long before I noticed something that really interested me. A large percentage of the men coming to the Home were prison inmates who were transitioning, or trying to transition, back into society. At the halfway house, they were halfway there.

I took a special interest in these men and wanted to do whatever I could to help them succeed. I got to know them very well, because I was actually living with them. Being the Director of the Home gave me a much different perspective that I'd had when I was merely a member of the Board.

I found them fascinating. Empathy and compassion are only really possible when you can see yourself in the other person. When you can identify with them. By actually living in the Home, I could see at a very personal level that the residents were simply men like me. This was another confirmation of the fact that there are not two kinds of people.

In the recovery community you meet a lot of extreme people. It's almost a requirement for admission. Doyle was a gangster. Not a movie character, but the real thing. He was the product of an arranged marriage between two mafia families. Literally a prince of the underworld. He'd robbed twenty-two banks, run marijuana in to the west coast in five-ton shipments, and made heroin deals in Amsterdam. He'd then had a religious conversion in a Federal prison and was now trying to turn his life around.

It was tough going. Like me at one point in my life, he couldn't get a bank to let him have a checking account. "The people at First Citizen's won't even speak to me," he said. He'd robbed eight of them.

Another resident had robbed seventy-eight chicken restaurants. He too had leveraged the proceeds into a successful drug business. Like Doyle, he had experienced a religious conversion in prison and wanted to start a new life.

I had always been skeptical of jailhouse conversions. Not all the men that I met at the Home wanted to change, but a subset of them did, and I wanted to help them do it.

An idea began to form. Why not create a program to help prison inmates make the transition? Why not use their addiction and their membership in the recovery community as assets to help in this process? After all, my own alcoholism had proven to be the cornerstone for my new life.

This started my work on what I would call the Inmate Transition Program. This was an initiative that would occupy the next several years of my life and would enrich me in ways that I could not possibly have imagined.

∞∞∞∞∞∞

The Tar River Players produced *To Kill a Mockingbird*. I had always appreciated this play, as it was a Southern story, written by a Southerner, which addressed the problem of racism.

Racism is a human problem, rather than merely a Southern problem, but it was also an issue that I had with myself that I wanted to address. As a provincial, white, southern male, born in the first part of the 20th Century, I do not pretend that an unreasoning prejudice against the black race does not exist in me. It is not something that was "done to" me, nor is it something that I can simply will away. It is a problem which requires a spiritual answer, just as my alcoholism did. I hoped that participating in this play would help with that. It did, by helping me to become more conscious (and open) about my own shortcomings.

I was cast as Walter Cunningham, a member of a lynch mob that was turned back by having to explain to a young white girl what they were doing. As Walter, I was the man that led the mob away. Playing this role had a profound effect on me.

∞∞∞∞∞

While working on the play, I also continued to work on the Inmate project. I told Steve Franklin about what I was doing, and he became a supporter. The Session at Thomas Memorial voted to provide financial help for my work, and the project became a line item in the church's budget for that year.

I applied for a grant from the New Hope Presbytery, and they too provided much needed financial support.

I began work on a grant application for funds from the Governor's Crime Commission. For that, I would need the application to come from a nonprofit organization that would receive the funds and house the administration of the project. I approached some of the Board members at the Christian Fellowship home, and found them receptive to the idea. I also began to garner political support in Raleigh.

The Home's Director recovered from his surgery and returned to work. This brought with it the gift of yet another perspective of what went on at the Home. I had been (and still was) a member of the Board. I had served as Director of the Home during the regular Director's absence. Now I was a resident, living among the men and working on the Inmate Project. It didn't take long for me to become uneasy with what I saw about the way the Home was run.

Residents were forbidden to have jobs that would prevent them from being present at an in-house meeting that the Director had arranged, even if this resulted in their being unable to pay their rent and losing their bed. This meeting was not essential to the men's sobriety, or their spiritual growth (no single meeting is). This was an arbitrary decision on the part of the Director. There was no appeal except to the Board, and the Board *never* went against the wishes of the Director. I knew this, having served as a Board member.

Residents who had skills in carpentry, electrical work, or other trades were required to provide their services to the home without compensation or reduction in their rent. Even if this work took them away from their paying jobs. The Director also used men from the Home to work on his own home, paying them a fraction of the pay that they would receive on their regular jobs.

One night I had a dream in which I saw a train derailed. The scene was a catastrophic train wreck. A voice (which I now know as the voice of God) said, "You will not be able to work from the inside."

The next day I was in the Director's office when he got a call from a State mental health facility. The Director agreed to provide a bed for a mentally ill man who was being discharged from the hospital.

The man arrived, dropped off by a social worker from the hospital. After the social worker left, the Director learned that the man was receiving a disability check, which would have to be considered in any application for work that the man might make. This violated one of the Director's unwritten rules, and the man was ordered to leave the premises immediately. This order was enforced by a 260 pound "house man" who served as a supervisor of the residents.

A mentally ill man had been put out on the streets a strange city with no access to medical resources or support whatsoever.

This was yet another turning point that I had no choice about. I confronted the Director, and when I got nowhere with him, I packed my bags and left. The dream I'd had played out in my waking life.

Bob Kelly agreed to let me come back to his place. "Short term only," he said gravely.

I called my cousin Jack, the relative who had helped me out by arranging my year-long stay at Robindale years before. Once again he stepped up. He allowed me to move into a spare house that he had in his front yard. No one had lived in the house for several years and it was being used for storage. I moved in and "camped out" there, while continuing to work on the Inmate Project.

A couple of weeks later, there was a tapping on my bedroom window at 2:00 am. It was Art Radley, whom I'd met at the Fellowship Home. Art had been put out of the Home for two weeks for violating one of the house rules. He'd tracked me down by talking to Wiley James, one of the other residents, whom I'd helped find work with a timber-framing company in Tarboro. Art was at his wits end and in tears.

"Where can I go?" he cried.

"You'll stay here with me," I said at once. His surprise at that was genuine.

"That really hadn't occurred to me," he said. I *knew* that he was telling me the truth. Art moved in, which was easy since he had everything that he owned in the world in his knapsack. We talked about recovery, and I started moving him toward a 4th Step.

Wiley James got Art a job interview at the timber-framing business where he was working. Wiley was an artisan woodworker. Art couldn't match Wiley's skill level, but he was a big strong man, and he was willing to work. That proved to be enough to get him hired.

My cousin Jack stopped me in the yard one afternoon and asked me, "What's that other guy doing here?" I explained that Art was a recovering drug addict and that I was working with him to get him straightened around. "Look," said Jack, "I can hide you here, but I don't know about him."

Hide me?, I thought. I got the same interior sensation that I'd gotten when Hank had asked me to sign that letter. By now I'd learned to trust that ineffable nothing. As soon as Jack left, I went downtown. I went to my old office building on Saint James Street. The place had been closed up for six years. The building has no street frontage. Entrance is gained through alleyways, one coming from Saint James Street and a second one from the parking lot in back of the fertilizer company next door. There was no running water, but for some unexplainable reason the lights were on. There was no electric meter on the building.

I went to Cousin Jack's office, which was across the alley from my front door, and told him that I was moving into the old office building to live.

When I told Art what we were going to do, he looked amazed and a little afraid, but he agreed.

Chapter 14

The Hermit
April 2007

...But above all, take it one day at a time.
Bill Wilson

The next morning, Art went to his job, and I went downtown.
The building was a filthy mess. It was filled with a combination of the
carnage left from the collapse of my business and my personal effects
which had been sitting there since my eviction from my apartment.
The first thing I needed was a water source.

Situated as the building is, in an alley system and away from the
street front, my front door looks out at the back doors of my
neighbors. There is the back door of a law office, the back door of
Cousin Jack's office, the back door of a jewelry store, and the back
door of an apartment that fronts on Main Street.

The apartment was occupied by a young lawyer who was an AA
friend. He kindly agreed to give me free access to his laundry room
where I could fill milk jugs with water and carry them over to my
place.

I filled the reservoir of the toilet on the second floor so that I
could have one flush when needed, then proceeded to the third floor.
My idea was to rehabilitate the building from the top down.

The third floor had been a call center for my business. There was
one large room, roughly 800 square feet, and a smaller employee break
room that was about 200 square feet. It was filled with derelict office
furniture and fixtures.

Movable panels had been used to construct cubicles for computer-assisted call stations. Now the panels were upended, and chairs, desks, and the carcasses of old computer systems were scattered everywhere.

A small window in the room had been broken out and birds had made homes on this floor. This I knew to be a serious health issue, so I went and got a good supply of the strongest cleaners that I could find and gave the whole room a thorough cleaning. This was going to be my main living area.

The old break room would be my kitchen. There was a small sink, that was dry at this point, a folding table that had come from one of the local Baptist churches, and more rubble.

I got some large trash bags and began ferrying debris down the stairs and out to the trash receptacles in the alley.

When Art got home from work, we made some space on the second floor for him to sleep. He would use a daybed that I'd brought from the apartment.

Then we moved the divider panels out of the big room on the third floor. This was not as hard a job as it might have been, since my building was constructed as an addition to my cousin Sam's business. The two buildings shared a wall, so all Art and I had to do was carry the big panels through a door and down three steps to the building next door. Sam's building was vacant, so I used it for storage. For the time being. We brought my microwave oven up from the second floor, along with some boxes of kitchen utensils and organized the kitchen a little.

Next we reassembled my bed, which had been waiting for me since my eviction from the apartment. We placed it facing east, with the headboard against the west wall. It is still in that same spot.

I made the bed up, got into it, and went to sleep. I slept soundly. I was no longer homeless.

The next morning, I did my morning devotionals and got Art off to work after a breakfast of peanut butter sandwiches.

Then, I heated a bowl of water in the microwave and shaved and bathed myself standing at the kitchen sink. I'd read somewhere that sailors had done things this way when they were living in conditions with a limited supply of water. I would have plenty of time to get used to this routine, since I was months away from having running water, and a full year away from a regular bath.

I spent the rest of the day cleaning and organizing my new home. When Art came home from work, we made a grocery run for microwavable food and other items, buying only things that didn't require refrigeration. We then moved two big bookcases up from the second floor. They had been office furniture until then. I unpacked and shelved my library. Books have been good friends to me my whole life. They have helped me get where I needed to go. I had really missed them. I had a tiny TV set with a built-in VCR player. We watched a mindless action flick and went to bed.

The days processed. We brought my art collection to the third floor and hung it. The furniture from my previous dwelling was arranged and a really nice loft apartment began to emerge from the chaos.

Although summer had not arrived, it was on the way, and things were getting hot. The business' big central air conditioner wasn't working, and the window units on the second floor had been carried away during the dissolution of the company.

Art and I cannibalized the old 40's era heating system on the second floor and took out a big squirrel-cage fan. We mounted it facing outward from a window at the end of the kitchen and we had a homemade attic fan that would pull a huge volume of air through the building. Fortunately, I was old enough to remember life before air conditioning and knew we'd be ok. Not overly comfortable, but we'd live, and, I'd gotten the world's best kitchen exhaust fan in the bargain.

∞∞∞∞∞∞

"All of us have sinned, and fallen short of the glory of God," said Steve Franklin.

Actually, that's not true, I thought to myself. *That's not even possible. Not if God is everything.*

"All of us have things that we wish that we could go back and say or do differently," said Steve.

Wrong again, I thought. *If I hadn't been there, I wouldn't be here.*

Steve was performing the Holy Eucharist. The Communion Service. I didn't take Communion anymore. I didn't say the Lord's Prayer, I didn't recite the Creeds, and there were more and more of the hymns that I couldn't sing anymore.

Back in the early 90s, I'd stopped going to church, and sworn that I'd never return. Then I'd had a couple of powerful dreams. Neither of the dreams was very long, but they had changed my life.

In the first dream, I was looking out from Thomas Memorial at Saint James Street. It was dark, and I saw a curved pathway with lights bordering it, leading to where I was standing. The lights reminded me of airport taxiway lights.

The second dream came a few nights later. In this dream, I was standing on Saint James Street, across the street from the Church, looking at the building. It was dark again, and I was holding a .300 Weatherby Magnum Rifle. The shadow of a deer flew between me and the church, and I swung the rifle and fired. The shot hit a stained glass window. The window was where I had been standing in the first dream. The bullet went through a figure of Jesus holding a lamb, then went all the way through the Church.

I spent a good bit of time talking about the dream with Robert Heatherly, and he'd had me go down to the Church and examine the window. Like all of the Church's windows, it's beautiful. The dedication is to a faithful member of the church who served as the Superintendent of the Sunday school for many years. All of the windows are now covered with Plexiglas shields that were added at the insistence of the insurance company. One of the church members told me that this was, "to protect the Church against acts of God." Plexiglas won't stop a .300 Magnum though.

Thomas Memorial, which is named after my great-grandparents, is a "country club" church. Of course my mother, who was an Episcopalian, was positive that no Presbyterian church could ever be on the same level that her church was, but it was still a high-caste, "deep pockets" congregation. As a boy, I'd been a "child of the church". Eventually I'd joined and had become a member. I was "one of us". Life had taken me on a great adventure, and at some point members of the Church had stopped being "us" and had become "them". I'd also developed what Robert Heatherly called a "reaction formation" against the Church, against Christianity, and against the part of society I'd come from. I had a problem.

"I don't know where the answers to your questions are," Robert had told me, "but I promise you that some part of them are over there (with 'them') somewhere." I decided to try going back to church.

It was the Christmas season, and Steve was preaching on Matthew 25, wherein God separates the sheep from the goats. The sheep of course get eternal life, but the goats are cast "into the fire that I have prepared for the devil and his angels".

I thought at once of a Jesus saying from The Gospel of Thomas, 'He who is near to me is near the fire, and he who is far from me is far from the Kingdom.'[7] There was no goat in the Church's manger

---

[7]Willis Barnstone, ed., "The Gospel of Thomas, 82", The Other Bible, HarperCollins Publishers, New York, NY

scene. *These people need a goat!,* I thought. *I'm a goat. I've always been a goat. I live in the fire.*

I started going to Church. I went to the regular worship service, to Sunday school, and to the Tuesday morning Men's Bible Study. The Sunday school and the Bible Study were both good for me, but the regular worship service less so. I would find it more and more unacceptable until it finally dropped off altogether.

∞∞∞∞∞

When I came home from Bible Study one Tuesday morning, I found my cousin Jack in the alley with the Town's Electric Department. Not someone from the Department, but the whole Department. I asked one of the workers, "I there anyone back at the office?"

"One person to answer the phone," he replied. "This is pretty much everyone else."

Jack is on the Town Council, and he enjoys his work there immensely. Now he'd used his power to call out an entire municipal department to help him try to micromanage my life. The supervisor, with Jack looking over his shoulder, was examining the connection between my building and the power line. They found that when the meter had been pulled off the building six years before, the electricity simply arced over and made a connection that had been flowing, unmetered, for six years while the building had been empty. It had been waiting for my return.

The supervisor cut the power and told me that I'd have to install a new junction box before it could be restored. As he was speaking, I looked over his shoulder, and saw an electrician's work van in the parking lot behind him.

I found the electrician working in the building next to mine. When he finished his work there, he came over and installed the junction box for me. I called the Town Hall and power was restored.

The electrician gave me a bill for his work. I didn't know how I'd be able to pay it, but a month later, the Men's Bible Study group took up an unsolicited collection for me that gave me enough money to pay the electrician, with enough left to call a plumber.

When my building had been added to the original structure, the plumbing was done as a simple extension of the existing plumbing. The part that I bought had never had a water meter. When Sam's part of the structure had been undermined by the Great Flood of '99, it had been abandoned. My part was not as badly damaged and was still usable.

I found the plumber who had taken care of the old building. He inspected the original connection, cut off the plumbing to all but my part of the structure, and gave me the "go ahead". The Town changed the account name on the meter to mine and turned it on. Water flowed to the sinks and toilets on the first and second floor, and to the sink in my kitchen on the third floor.

I was then able to use a detachable hookup to connect an old washer/dryer stack to the bathroom sink. These appliances had been stored in my building by my friend Eddie-Rock Denton when he'd lost his house. The Rock had gone back to drugs one time too many. He'd tripped and fallen, choking to death on his dentures on a friend's living room floor. His death had left a sizable hole in my life.

I could now do a cold water wash, catching the waste water in buckets as it came out of the drain hose and emptying them in the toilet (I had been using the Church's laundry before this).

There had never been any hot water in my building, except for a five-gallon supply in the old break room (which no longer worked). When he'd built his new office, old Mr. Clark had thought of hot water as an unnecessary extravagance.

There was no shower or bathtub yet, but I was very happy to no longer have to "carry my own water" for bathing, washing dishes, and flushing the toilet.

Something woke me up late one night and I found Art going through my dresser drawer searching for money for drugs. When I asked what he was up to, he ran.

He called the next day. "I guess I fucked up," he said.

"I guess you did," I said simply. There was nothing to be mad about, but he had to go. I was living by myself again. Art and I remain friends.

∞∞∞∞∞∞

The Tar River Players agreed to present *Inherit the Wind*. The idea to do this play was mine. My friend Jim Jefferson, "on board" at once, agreed to direct the play. We took the idea to the planning committee, they signed off on it, and we were on our way.

Inherit the Wind, written by Jerome Lawrence and Robert E. Lee, is not history. It was, however, inspired by the events that took place in Dayton, Tennessee in 1925 at the celebrated Scopes "Monkey Trial". The trial was a "battle of giants" that pitted the famous (or infamous) trial lawyer Clarence Darrow against the popular orator William Jennings Bryan. The issue was Biblical authority. The acceptance of the Christian Bible as a literal account of historical events.

Having been sired by a man who lived his life in accord with an unbending literal interpretation of the Bible, I had come to realize that this issue was a part of the conflict that I'd had with my father. I now believe it was a big part of the reason that I'd been unable to remain in his house. He really hadn't wanted to throw me out, but I had insisted. I'd behaved in such a way that eventually he'd been *forced* to "cast me out". There are a number of parallels in the Bible, stories of "the rejected son". So many in fact, that I've been able to find a great deal of meaning for my own journey from the stories of these other "rejected sons".

When Ishmael and his mother are cast out by Abraham, they are barely out of sight before Isaac is being referred to as Abraham's "only son". The resemblance of this account to the account of Jehovah's casting out of his other son is apparent.

I think it's easy to see that casting someone out doesn't mean that they no longer exist, and that they aren't, in fact, still part of the family. The main source of my ongoing irritation with Jehovah is his failure to reconcile himself with his own rejected son. If he can't deal with his own family, why should I concern myself with him?

I had never seen the play, but I had seen the movie several times, and had been thrilled by it. It spoke to me all the way down to my bones. Brian and I began to work to drum up support and enthusiasm for the project.

My living space was looking pretty good by now, and we decided to have an "*Inherit the Wind* Party". We arranged to rent an 84 inch television to show the movie and invited everyone we knew. As the party drew closer, it occurred to me that my space, big as it was, might not accommodate everyone that might show up. There was, however, a perfect solution to that problem close at hand.

I contacted the head of the nonprofit development company that owned the old mercantile company's building that my space was attached to. There was a door next to my bed that opened into a sixty-foot-square "bullpen" office on the second floor of the old building. The Great Flood hadn't touched the second floor offices, which had been some of the nicest in Tarboro. They were musty but perfectly usable.

"Mary, what we'd like to do is clean that room up, use it to show a movie to a bunch of people, clean it up again, and leave. You're invited to come too!" I told her.

"Sounds ok to me," she replied cheerfully.

The day before the party was to happen I was working with the theater company's female stage-manager cleaning up the big space when I heard footsteps and voices coming up from the floor below. I met the City Planner and the Building Inspector as they came in. "We don't know what to do with your cousin Jack," they said. I showed them the big space and explained what we were doing, and assured them that we had permission. "You're in violation of the city code doing this," they said ruefully. "Our hands are really tied. You simply can't do it." I assured them that we wouldn't and that I understood perfectly where they were coming from.

Roberta Cashwell, the theater company's Producer, wanted to cancel the party, but I talked her into letting me move the party back into my space. "It'll work out," I promised her. "Don't let him do this to us."

The party went better than I expected. I didn't count the people, but my place was filled to capacity. There was laughter. People came and went on the top two floors, and my friends admired my running water.

The movie was preceded by a cartoon. *The Mask Man*, Lenny Bruce's classic underground parody on the Lone Ranger.

The night's feature was much appreciated. Afterwards, the core of the theater group stayed around and talked. There was enthusiasm. It was time to start moving on the production.

Bob Kelly I and started beating the bushes for props. We found what we needed without going too far, and some of the items that were used as props during the play eventually found their way back to my home to be used as furnishings.

Some items that we found went directly to my place without making an appearance on stage. In my cousin Joe Braswell's barns we found an old claw-foot bathtub, an enormous 85 gallon electric water heater, an ancient refrigerator, and an old electric stove. I asked him if

187

I could have them, and Joe said, "Sure, take them. Actually I'm not sure who left that stove out there, so if I come and ask for that back, no hard feelings."

The tub and the water heater went to the second floor. There was no plumbing to accommodate either of them, but there was the promise of future bathing.

The old stove and refrigerator went to the kitchen. My friend George Smith ran an eight foot wire from a junction box, put in a stove receptacle, and I was cooking again!

Rehearsals started. I was cast as Henry Drummond, the Clarence Darrow "lookalike", who was seen by the community as either "an atheist", or "the Devil", or both. My opponent in the courtroom was Matthew Harrison Brady, the darling of the community, and a proponent of "that old time religion". This was unfinished business for me. Both with my long-dead father and with the Church.

> Brady said to Drummond, "We were good friends
> once. I was always glad of your support. What
> happened between us? There used to be a mutuality of
> understanding and admiration. Why is it, my old
> friend that you have moved so far away from me?"
> I replied, "All motion is relative. Perhaps it is *you*
> who have moved away – by standing still."

I absolutely loved being Henry Drummond, and had no trouble whatsoever learning my lines. I was on stage for most of the play after the first act and there was a lot of dialogue, but I felt at home. All I had to do was be myself.

∞∞∞∞∞∞

George Smith was living in an apartment across the alley from me that was owned by my cousin Joe Braswell. He was running a woodworking shop two blocks away in the old Sullivan Building on Main Street. My cousin Joe was involved in the shop too.

When he was not at the shop, George spent part of his time helping me renovate my living space. "Farm boy" George had been reared with an education that included carpentry, plumbing, and electrical work, in addition to his college degree. He had skill sets that were completely absent from my own resume.

I had a licensed electrician add a circuit for the water heater, then George hooked it up. We got some PVC from Lowe's, and he plumbed in hot water to all the sinks. Then he and his helper Alex put the old claw-foot tub in place, connected it to the water lines, and I had the most elegant bath that anyone has ever taken.

We pulled an old 220 volt air conditioner out of a window on the first floor. The unit had been partially submerged in the Great Flood, but when George tested it, he found that it worked. Installed in a kitchen window, and augmented by a couple of large fans, it made the third floor much more habitable in the summertime.

∞∞∞∞∞

I got a phone call from my son Jack. Jack had been diagnosed as a paranoid schizophrenic when he was about 20, and for the last ten years he'd had a really wild ride. He'd gone to prison for larceny, been six times to Cherry Hospital (one of the State's facilities for mental illness), and had actually been invited to leave the State of Tennessee. I'd tried everything I could think of to help, but with no success. The problem that couldn't be overcome was Jack's denial that he had a problem. He didn't believe that he had schizophrenia, and it is impossible to help anyone who doesn't know that he has a problem.

189

"Dad, I don't want to be disabled," Jack told me when he called. "I want to work, to get a job, and get an apartment."

How can I not help with that? I picked him up at the assisted living facility where he'd been staying and brought him home with me. We set up a bedroom on my second floor. I arranged for Jack's disability checks to come to me and arranged with a local therapist to treat him as often as we could work out sessions. Jim Winslow, a local doctor and childhood friend, helped with prescriptions for medication.

Jack came home badly overmedicated. Many of the facilities like the one in which he'd been staying would overmedicate their residents in order to make them easier to manage. The one where he had been living had followed this practice. He'd been doped to the gills to make him compliant. For virtually the entire time that Jack had been sick the approach to his treatment had been entirely pharmacological, with no provision for therapeutic sessions with a psychologist. I was trying to change that. The sessions with the local therapist began and I began to wean Jack off of most of the medicines that he'd been taking, leaving his primary antipsychotic drug in place. Jack spent most of his time smoking cigarettes, drinking soft drinks, and exploring the town where he grew up. Cousin Jack immediately put up "No Smoking" signs on his side of the alley. I responded in the spirit of mature Southern manhood by asking all of my guests to, "Please restrict your smoking to the designated No Smoking area."

I worked on improving Jack's diet, and gradually, under the guidance of my doctor friend, began reducing the dosage of the antipsychotic drug. Jack's general health was surprisingly good considering the life that he'd been leading and the massive amounts of medicine that he'd been taking for years.

Therapy continued. There was a little improvement. Jack seemed happy and agreed to participate in a program in Rocky Mount designed to give him the ability to function in a community.

There were setbacks too. I tried giving Jack the money from his disability check. Jack took the money and immediately disappeared for two days and nights to smoke the money up on crack cocaine and do some business with the local crack whores.

My friend Art had spent much time in the same fashion and it had baffled me. Not that I didn't understand addiction, I did. What I didn't understand was how I could live in the same community, walk the same streets, and not see the prostitutes. It was still another parallel universe. Where were they? I remembered a conversation that I'd once had with my old business partner Hank who'd been telling me about a revival preacher from Greenville who'd shown up with a whore at a card game. Hank had been his usual eloquent self.

> The preacher brought a whore to the game with him.
> She really was something. I could go to the Baltimore
> Airport, and in an hour find twenty whores who would
> look less like a whore than that whore.

I still didn't know what to look for, but ever since Hank told me that, whenever I pass through the Baltimore Airport I look at every woman there and wonder.

There were ups and downs. Finally at 2:30 one morning, Jack had a psychotic break. I awoke to find my son running through the house stark naked. He told me that there were people chasing him. I didn't see any other people.

I got Jack to sit on the daybed on the second floor, and we had one of the best conversations that we'd had in years. Sitting there naked, Jack admitted that he had the disease he'd always vehemently denied. He talked much more lucidly about himself and his life, staying in the present rather than retreating into the long-gone past of his childhood.

I called the police who came at once. Jack got dressed and was taken to Nash Hospital in Rocky Mount. From there he went to the

191

Coastal Plain Hospital where he was once again given medication and returned to Tarboro.

He was back, but still not stable. One evening, the police called me and said that Jack had called 911 and reported that I had shot him in the ear. The officer asked if he could bring him home, and I said, "Yes." Two cops and Jack were there in ten minutes. They sat and talked. Jack told them that yes, I had shot him.

"Not shot at you, but actually shot you?" one of the officers asked.

"Yes," confirmed Jack.

I told the officers that since Jack was convinced that I had shot him he obviously couldn't stay with me. "If he sees me attacking him, it would only be natural for him to defend himself. Anyone would do that." The officers agreed.

The weather outside was terrible. There was a blinding snowstorm and the roads were as slick as glass. "Normally we would take him to Nash Hospital in Rocky Mount," the senior officer said. "But with the weather like it is we're going to take him to Heritage here in Tarboro. Can you follow us there?"

"Sure," I replied.

Arriving at the ER, the officers completed the necessary paperwork and went back to work. I waited for an hour, then asked a nurse if I could speak to the doctor. "There's been a bad wreck," the nurse replied. "Everybody's got more than they can handle right now. I would guess that it'll be at least two hours before any of the doctors can speak to you." I gave the nurse on the desk my phone number and asked that the doctor call me when that became possible. Then I went home.

It was only 8:30, but I got ready for bed and curled up with a book. I soon fell asleep with the book on my chest. I was awakened by the phone ringing at about 9:30. "Mr. Thomas, this is Doctor

Tammy Roberts," said a curt female voice, "I'm here with your son. Can you tell me why you brought him out here?"

I was wide awake now. "Actually I didn't take him out there. The police did. He's there because he's psychotic."

"I know that," the doctor snapped, "but that doesn't make him committable."

"He thinks I shot him," I explained "not shot at him, but actually shot him."

"I know that," the doctor said, "I've been talking with him and he tells me he's fine now. I have his entire record here in front of me."

"I don't think you can have his entire record there." I countered, "This has been going on for years. He's been admitted to psychiatric hospitals all over the place, in two states in fact. That includes six trips to Cherry Hospital and one stay in the medical unit at Central Prison."

"The fact is, he's not committable," said the doctor, heatedly. "Can he be taken back to your house?"

"Of course not!" I said in exasperation. "He is a paranoid schizophrenic that thinks I've tried to kill him!"

"Mr. Thomas, I think that you are a very angry man and I'm going to pray for you," steamed the Doctor.

At this I saw red, but said as calmly as I could manage, "Well Doctor, I find you to be very arrogant!"

"I am not arrogant," said Doctor Roberts, now barely in control of herself. "I am one of the most humble people that I know! If you saw me on the street downtown, you wouldn't even be able to tell that I was a doctor!"

As mad as I was, I almost burst out laughing. "What did you say?" I asked in amazement.

"I *said*," she repeated, "that I am one of the most humble people that I know. If you saw me on the street somewhere, you wouldn't even be able to tell that I'm a doctor!" I was too amazed to speak, but the doctor was on a roll. "I think you're a very angry man," she said again, "and I'm going to pray for you!"

The "pray for" hit my hot button again and I said, "Doctor, I've gone way past anger now."

"You're very angry and I'll pray for you," she said for the third time.

"Well fuck you, bitch!" I stormed. That ended the conversation.

She called back in about a half hour. "Mr. Thomas, this is Doctor Tammy Roberts." I said nothing. "I cannot put your son out in this weather," she said heatedly. "I'm going to send him to Cherry Hospital, but only because of the weather."

"Thank you," I said, and hung up.

"She did not say that!" said my friend Worth Houston when I gleefully told him about the humble doctor the next morning. Worth was the President of the Hospital and a friend from the Tar River Players.

"Did too," I laughed. "The only thing is Worth, this is a small town. I'm bound to run into her somewhere!"

"I wouldn't worry about that," Worth replied, smiling through the phone. "You won't be able to tell she's a doctor."

This "weather-related" commitment lasted for four months of inpatient treatment at the Goldsboro facility. After his release, the hospital sent Jack a bill for over $164,000 which, of course, he could not pay. After this he went through a period of relative stability at an assisted living facility in Johnston County which allowed his family to enjoy having him home to visit again.

Since that time, Jack has had many more ups and downs that have included more jail time and more visits to Cherry Hospital. At this writing, Jack is a resident of another group home based in Johnston County. He has been there for about two years and is doing very well. I am very proud of my son.

I was going to AA, and I was going to the Church. There was a Discovery Class in the Sunday School that I particularly enjoyed. Steve and I had a number of very fine talks during this time. I found many wonderful people at the Church. Even though I'd known many of them for my whole life, I found that I was seeing them differently and really enjoying being around them.

Steve was a particular joy. A real man. From the standpoint of theology there were many differences. These didn't bother me. *Without Contraries is no progression.*[8] I was very conscious of the fact that my friend was helping me to solidify my own beliefs.

The Discovery Class studied *The Gospel of Thomas*, which I had been reading and enjoying for years. The fact that Thomas is not a narrative gospel, but a series of "sutra-like" teachings was pleasing.

Life was very good.

I reached the age of 62 and Social Security kicked in. There was not much money, but my overhead was so low that it was enough.

George Smith "needed a little space" from Joe Braswell and took one of my second floor bedrooms. We continued making improvements to the house. Wonderful light fixtures came from George's Uncle Randolph's barn. Container gardening was initiated in the alley with George making planters from scrap wood at the shop. A new arrangement of interior lights for the living room showed my art collection to much better effect.

After a time, George moved on. He closed the woodshop and went back into the business world that he'd known before. This involved providing a front-end processing system for personal-injury lawyers. This work wouldn't suit me at all, but it was George's forte. He was very, very good at it and this synergy attracted connections

---

[8] David V. Erdman, ed., "The Marriage of Heaven and Hell", *The Complete Poetry & Prose of William Blake,* Bantam Doubleday Dell Publishing Group, Inc., New York, NY

and money. He moved back into the apartment building that he'd been in before the Great Flood and begin to thrive.

∞∞∞∞

One morning, I found a notice for a registered letter in my mailbox. In the old days this would have really scared me. The only reason that I would have gotten such a notice was to notify me of trouble with the IRS or some other legal problem. Now it made me a little nervous, but nothing like it would have fifteen years before.

I walked straight to the Post Office and got the letter, telling the clerk that it was "usually some kind of invitation." It certainly was. The letter was from a man named Daniel Simpson who said that he was my son! There was a picture enclosed and the resemblance was enough to remove any doubts I might have had.

From the letter I knew that this was a child that I had fathered in the back seat of a '64 Chevy after an American Legion dance in 1965. My parents had found out, of course. I had never really known what had happened after that, as such things were never talked about in my father's house. They were disallowed. It just wasn't going to happen. The expectant mother had simply disappeared from the face of the earth. From their attitude toward unlicensed sex and the results of such activities, I had believed that there had been an abortion. Obviously I'd been wrong.

I had run into Daniel's mother a few years before on a Main Street sidewalk. I hadn't recognized her and she was too angry, understandably so, for us to have had a conversation even if I'd wanted to, which I hadn't.

The letter was friendly enough and gave me three options as to how I might respond. The first option was to do nothing, to not acknowledge the event. The second would be to provide a family medical history, which would be of value to the man I'd fathered in dealing with health issues, but to have no other interaction with him. The third option was to contact Daniel Simpson. I picked up my phone and called.

In a few weeks, Daniel made a trip to Tarboro to meet his father. We talked in my living room.

Daniel had actually been born in Edgecombe General Hospital in Tarboro, about two weeks earlier than my son Chris was born in Pitt Memorial Hospital in Greenville.

He was then adopted by a couple in Greensboro and reared by them in a loving household.

Daniel was an insurance salesman by profession and was one of the most conservative fundamentalist Christians that I had ever encountered. His adoptive parents were Presbyterian, but Daniel had rejected this path because his studies indicated that the Presbyterian Church was not "Bible-based", but was based instead on the Westminster Confession of Faith. I didn't argue this issue with him. I wouldn't have even if I could have. Daniel was now a grown man and had his own path to follow.

It was not lost on me, however, that I now had a son who considered the Bible to be the authority for his life. I was at the far end of the spectrum from Daniel with respect to "Biblical Authority". I find the mainstream church's idolatrous relationship to the Bible to be one of its two biggest problems. There was something about this extreme dichotomy between Daniel and myself that I found strangely comforting.

Daniel liked Tarboro. In fact, he liked it so much that he rented a house about four blocks away from me and lived there for a year in order to get to know both me and his birth mother, who was still in town. Eventually he returned to the Greensboro area to continue his journey.

∞∞∞∞

After this, I had several business initiatives that did not work. That didn't bother me too much. As long as I could honestly tell myself that I'd given the idea my best shot I was ok either way. *It's not whether you win or lose, but how you play the game.* At any rate, there was nothing that could be "won" in the objective sense that could compare to what I'd already found inside myself. And what I had found could never be "lost". This Reality was reflected outward into the world. "For the kingdom of the Father is already spread out over the earth," Jesus had said, "but people don't see it.[9]"

The lack of a mate did bother me. I tried connecting with several women, but there was no spark. I thought of the latter chapters of Hesse's *Narcissus and Goldmund*[10], when the spark between Goldmund and the women he encountered faded. *Maybe that part of my life is over,* I thought. *Well, if that's the case, I certainly have nothing to complain about. God has already given me more than my share of everything.*

I shared my lament with Jim Jefferson. "Women just don't like locusts and wild honey," I told him sadly. "I really don't want to spend the rest of my life as some kind of eccentric hermit."

"But you're so good at it!" Jim enthused, grinning from ear to ear.

---

[9] Willis Barnstone, ed., "The Gospel of Thomas", 113, *The Other Bible*, HarperCollins Publishers, New York, NY

[10] Hesse, Hermann. *Narcissus And Goldmund.* New York: Picador 1930

Chapter 15

The Lover
March 2010

For one human being to love another human being: that is
the most difficult task that has been entrusted to us...
the work for which all other work is merely preparation.
                                    - Rainer Maria Rilke

Gilgamesh is an old story. In fact it is sometimes referred to as "the oldest story in the world". It is the story of a tyrant king who ruled in Mesopotamia nearly 5,000 years ago.

Reports came to the king of a naked, very powerful, wild man who was terrifying inhabitants of the kingdom. In what might be called in AA a "moment of clarity", instead of sending troops to kill or capture the wild man, the normally violent king took a different tack. He sent a girl. Her job was not to harm the wild man, but to tame him and bring him to the king. This she did in the usual way.

Unlike the king, the wild man wasn't habitually violent. Enkidu was a child of nature who cared for and protected the animals. He was a mirror image of the king. When the men met, two very unexpected things happened. The wild man became *human*, and the king became *civilized* and was no longer a tyrant. There was peace at last. This transformation took place under the auspices of the temple priestess who had tamed the wild man.

Since the time of these legendary events, this same adventure has been recurring every hour of the day, all over the world. It is *exactly* what happened to me.

∞∞∞∞

I was at the Library one day and was having a computer problem. These problems seemed to happen fairly often to me, in spite of the fact that at one time in my life, I'd actually been an IT person. I asked for help, and the Reference Librarian was sent over.

She was an attractive young woman, with a name tag that said, "Dianne." I'd noticed her before at the Library, and had managed to get on the same walking tour that she was on on the last History Days Ghost Tour.

She attended to my computer problem without too much difficulty. By that time, I was feeling a strong attraction and was enjoying talking with her, so I kept the conversation going. I learned that her name was Dianne Baker, and that she was the Assistant Director of the Library. She was from Wilson, and *she was in the process of moving to Tarboro.*

She's coming my way!, I thought. We talked on. She was divorced and had three children. Only one of the children, a son, was still living at home. "He doesn't want to move to Tarboro," she said. "He says that there is no Starbuck's here, and that he's going to go and live with his father. I told him 'fine'. He can go ahead and try that, if that's what he wants to do."

My mind went instantly to the scene in one of the Star Wars movies where the young Anakin Skywalker was leaving home to do his Jedi training and his mother was letting him do it. *Wow!*, I thought. *This is a really strong woman.* She was smiling and walking away. I let her go, but knew I wanted to see her again.

The next day I was back at the Library. She was helping another patron, but when I got an opening, I walked over and said, "I've got another question for you, if you've got time." She did, so we started walking toward the computers. "Would you like to have lunch with me?" I asked. Her mouth dropped open, and we stopped walking.

200

She was obviously taken completely by surprise. We stood there for a minute looking at each other. *Its ok,* I thought. *I just surprised her.* "Would you like to think about it, and call me later?" I asked.

"Yes," she replied.

I walked to the Circulation Desk and got a piece of scratch paper and wrote down my name and phone number for her. "Call me when you get off work," I said. She agreed. *She's smiling,* I thought. *This is going to be ok.*

She called a little after 6:00 that afternoon, while she was driving home from work. "I'm sorry I couldn't talk earlier," she said. "Your invitation was so unexpected, I just didn't know what to say."

"That's no problem," I said. "Would you like to have lunch?"

"Yes," she said. Then, to my surprise, we continued to talk until she pulled into her driveway forty minutes later. She greeted her dog, who was waiting for her in her driveway, and I told her that I'd call the next day. I asked about her lunch hour. "I eat lunch at 1:00," she said.

The next morning, I made a 1:00 reservation at On the Square, Tarboro's "fine dining" place, which is located across the street from my place and gave her a call at the Library.

Lunch was great. The food was as good as always, and our conversation continued its easy flow. She had been born in California. Her father was a Navy officer, so she had moved around quite a bit, following in the wake of his career. "I've always lived on the edges of the Country," she said. "I can't imagine living in a state that doesn't border an ocean."

When I told her that I was in AA, I got a big surprise. "I am too!" she said. She had been sober for nine years. She had stopped going to meetings, and had focused her spiritual life on church for the last few years. "Actually, I've known for a while that I need a change," she said. "My daughter is gay. If I told the people at my church that, they'd start trying to fix her. I know for a fact that Lara isn't broken." The AA connection was the first of many signs, or pointers, that we were on the right track. Although nothing had been said yet, we both knew where things were going.

Her spiritual journey had been an ironic reversal of mine. As a small girl she had attended Self-Realization Fellowship, which had a Hindu founder. There, she sat in the lotus position chanting, "I am the bubble, make me the sea." She laughed, "What I was really thinking was 'I am a bubble, leave me alone.'"

From that beginning she had migrated though some mainstream Christian churches, spent time in AA, and finally landed in a small nondenominational church that was meeting in a converted public school in Wilson.

My journey had started in an orthodox church, then I married a witch and been a Unitarian.

After lunch, I invited her to walk through my place before going back to work. She liked it! When she saw the old bathtub, she said, "I love a bathtub. I never take showers." Another sign.

We began seeing each other every day. There were long walks and picnics on the Town Common. Nature took her course, and a few months later she moved in with me. She had an amazing dowry that included the three children (none in our home), a dog, and a working pinball machine.

With each passing day, my gratitude for the gift that I'd been given grew. Like all of us, Dianne had been wounded by life. At night, she would whimper in her sleep, tormented by the ghost of a past trauma. I would hold her and know that it was my job to provide her with a safe place to be. "Everyone turns to someone," Rumi had said. "Look for the one scarred by the king's polo stick."

I hurt her feelings once, over a family matter, to a point where she was brought to tears. This shocked and stopped me. I could see then that the tyrant *had* to be civilized.

In her first marriage, she had taken care of home and children while her husband worked. Now, she had a career, and I could have the role of homemaker. Fortunately, by this time in my life, I was pretty domesticated, and I had the imprint of my mother for a model.

∞∞∞∞

I got a call from Chris Rodrigues. Chris was a handsome young Puerto Rican man who had owned an art gallery in Tarboro during the time that I'd been living on Saint Patrick Street. I'd bought a lot of artwork from him for the apartment, and we'd become really close friends. His gallery had been washed away by the Great Flood and he was now living in New York. He was calling to tell me that he and his girlfriend Ha were getting married. He was going to take her back home to Puerto Rico for the wedding, and he wanted Dianne and me to come. I talked it over with Dianne. The trip would be a major commitment of time and money and I wasn't sure we could afford to go.

"Something tells me that this is something that we need to do," said Dianne. "It just feels that way to me. I know that we have a lot of stuff that needs doing here at home, but I've always thought that I'd rather do things than have things."

I called Chris to tell him that our plans were definite. "We got the tickets, so you and Ha can count on us."

"Awesome," Chris said. He hesitated then went on, "There is something I'd like to ask you to do for me." There was silence.

Finally I said, "You know I'll be happy to do whatever I can for you. What is it?"

"I don't know how to put it," Chris said tentatively. There was another long pause. Then he said, "We'd like for you to perform the ceremony for us." I was quiet. Of all the things I could have imagined that he might have asked for, that would not have occurred to me.

"I'm not credentialed," I finally said.

"I know that," Chris said. "I can have someone there to sign the paperwork. I just want you to do the words."

I thought for a minute then told him, "Of course. I'd be honored."

"How can you do that?" exclaimed Dianne when I told her. I explained that there would be someone on hand to "make things legal", but that I would be the one actually "blessing the union".

"Well I've never heard of anything like it," she said, then paused. "This is why I had such a strong feeling about it being the right thing to do," she finally said.

I really hate commercial air travel. It always feels like I'm being herded into a cattle car, and I can't help feeling that the Homeland Security people are the Gestapo. We got past all that, though, and had an amazing experience in Puerto Rico. The country was beautiful and the people were warm and welcoming. There was a Vietnamese Buddhist wedding ceremony to honor Ha's family's beliefs. The following afternoon, I conducted an American ceremony at Hacienda Siesta Alegre, an old home at the top of a mountain, overlooking the rainforest. It was one of the most beautiful places I've ever been, and one of the most amazing experiences that I've ever had.

∞∞∞∞

When I was running my business, I once had a visitor from Moscow. This was back when there was a Soviet Union. I showed the visiting consultant around Tarboro, and he said to me, "You have a nice village." That's what Tarboro is. A nice village.

Dianne and I continued the process of merging households and building a simple life. We live in the downtown district, so we rented a parking space to deal with Tarboro's "urban parking problem". The bank is across the street from our place. The Church, and also our AA meeting place, is two blocks away. The place where Dianne has her hair cut is two blocks away, and the City Barber Shop where my hair has been cut for over a half-century is only one. Dianne's commute to work is an eight minute walk.

Dianne began going to sessions with Robert Heatherly with me in Spartanburg, and we'd usually swing by and see my old AA sponsor, Sam Roundtree in Statesville as part of those trips.

The Jamboree, which is an annual AA retreat on Ocracoke Island, North Carolina became a regular event. The Jamboree is my favorite AA conference. It's held on the first full weekend in November, when the beach weather is good and the summer crowds have gone home. The speakers for the meetings are picked from the crowd, which I like much better than the semi-pro circuit speakers that I find at the larger conferences.

Dianne and I went to Sunday school and church and I continued my studies. The more time that passed, the greater distance there was between my spiritual life and the "faith of my fathers". Whether this was because I was moving faster, or because they were standing still didn't matter.

After Jesus' temptation in the desert, he'd come back and begun to preach, "The Kingdom of God is at hand." This is sometimes referred to as his first sermon. Everybody said, "That's great! When is it coming?" He tried telling them that the kingdom really was here a few more times, and when the crowds still didn't understand, he gave up and tried teaching with parables. They didn't understand those either.

Growing up at Thomas Memorial, I'd been told that we live in "a fallen and broken world". This belief was reinforced by people walking around wearing "the full armor of God" and singing about God as "a mighty fortress", "a bulwark never failing". This defensive posture it seems would continue in the Afterlife, when we arrived in Heaven to "find the streets are guarded by United States Marines".

My journey away from that fortress had begun more than twenty years before at the Getting the Love You Want conference in Asheville. I was startled by the fact that I'd not been able to see any of my parent's "negative" qualities. I was able to see then that I'd done the same thing with my concept of God. I talked about this problem with Robert Heatherly.

"Denial is not merely something that you refuse to think," he told me. "It's an unthinkable thought. There are some things that are simply unthinkable." I went to work at once on learning to think these "unthinkable" things.

The wife of Dave Best, one of my early AA sponsors, had died a horribly painful death from cancer. "God don't kill people," he would tell me. *Mine does,* I would think. *In fact, how else could I die?* "I trust You to kill me," Rumi had said.

Then I met Sam Roundtree, who would say to me, "The Book[11] says 'Either God is everything, or he's nothing'. Well if He's everything, that don't leave much."

Meister Eckhart told me,

> You might ask, "How can I know if something is
> God's will?" My answer is, "If it were not God's will,
> it wouldn't exist even for an instant; so if something
> happens, it *must* be his will."

Slowly, gradually, painfully, my concept of God expanded.

My studies of comparative religion showed me that there are some aspects of the Deity that are not included in the Christian pantheon. They are "cast out", or split off, as not being part of God.

---

[11] Reference to AA's Big Book

If God was to be whole, these other things had to be included as well. It's true that "God is love", but faith in love messes up faith in God.

Jung wrote about the mysterious role played by evil in delivering man from darkness and suffering.

William Blake said, "But in the Book of Job, Milton's Messiah is call'd Satan." In my own life, my soul had actually been saved by "demon rum". A new thought emerged in my mind. As time passed, it became more and more apparent to me. *There is no sin, and there is no death.*

The Church had told me that Jesus "conquered death", and that he was "The Lamb of God that takes away the sins of the world". Well, both death and the sins of the world were now gone for me. But whatever force had done these things in me bore no resemblance to the Sunday school Jesus that I'd been taught about.

∞∞∞∞

After a time, Robert Heatherly gently pushed me out of the nest. I had been seeing him for over twenty years, and moving on was difficult for me. He guided me to a Summer Dream Conference at the Haden Institute. The Conference is held at Kanuga, which is an Episcopal retreat center located between Spartanburg, SC and Asheville, NC. It is a "fellowship of men and women" on their individual spiritual quests. This fellowship is similar to AA, in that the spirituality there is *empirical.* That is to say, it is based on experience and observation, rather than on theory. As a person who has run his life guided by dreams and visions, I found another spiritual home. Dianne and I began attending these annual conferences, and I also enrolled in the Institute's Spiritual Direction Program. I didn't enroll in the Program in order to become a Spiritual Director, I did it in order to spend more time in the Haden Community.

This group of people, both faculty and students, is doing work that I think is vitally important. The cohort is about 40% clergy, and many of these priests are working to help their churches to see their own shadows.

In the realm of created things, every*thing* has a shadow. Wherever there is light, there is a shadow. The Taoists are right. Everything, and I do mean everything, contains the seed of its opposite. Assets become liabilities, blessings become curses, good becomes evil. Then, these things can change again and become what they had formerly been. There are no solids in the Universe. These priests at Haden (and all of us are priests) can help members of their churches to see that the two biggest obstacles on the road to an enlightened Christianity are Jesus and the Bible.

This *realization* is not an easy thing to get or have. It requires a lot of painful work, and no one, not even Jesus, can do it for you. God lives beyond time and space. Beyond good and evil. So, if you want to meet Him, you have to get out there with him. As Rumi said, "There is a field beyond wrongdoing and rightdoing. I'll meet you there." For this meeting, you will need the perspective of the cross. Not looking *at* the cross, but looking *from* the cross.

∞∞∞∞

Dianne and I were married on the second anniversary of her moving to Tarboro to make a home with me. The wedding took place at Jubilee! in Asheville. Jubilee! practices a Creation-Based Spirituality built to a large extent on the teachings of Matthew Fox. It is open, warm, and welcoming. I had been going there for years, whenever I had the opportunity, and the minister, Howard Hanger, had never once told me that I had sinned and fallen short of the glory of God.

Chris and Ha Rodrigues flew in from New York to witness our union. We had a wedding party of four.

Marriage is a sacrament that I am very much in favor of. Since I am a man who is "often married", I can tell you that it produces a very definite change in the chemistry of a relationship. Even if the couple has been living together for years. This has nothing to do with "living in sin". I know couples that have been married for forty years and have "lived in sin" the whole time. No, what that ceremony did for Dianne and me was to affirm something that had already happened, and take it to another, higher, level. I do honestly love all of my wives. Without their participation in my life, I could not possibly have the love that I have today. Never have I known such a joyous union, and never before in my life have I had anything like what I have with Dianne.

∞∞∞∞

Steve Franklin accepted a call to a larger church and moved on. He had enriched my life and I would miss him. After the incredibly long and convoluted process that the Presbyterian Church goes through to call ministers, he was replaced by Ben Kane. Ben is a "consummate Millennial" who brings new energy and a different chemistry to Thomas Memorial.

Jim Winslow, my childhood friend, began practicing medicine at the County's Department of Human Services, next door to my home. He had retired twice from the practice of medicine and now was working three days a week in answer to a call from God. He began coming next door to my place for lunch on his Tuesday lunch hour. We talk about his ministry with the Church Youth, his ministry with the economically disadvantaged population of Edgecombe County (we lead the State in incidences of several venereal diseases) and the annoyance that he shares with me with the "white-bearded old man" that we'd been given for a God. I really look forward to these enriching conversations each week.

He comes from a Quaker family that has lived in Tarboro for generations. Since there is no Friends meeting here, the Winslows attended the Presbyterian Church, but all of the boys (there were no girls) were sent off to Philadelphia ("Quaker Depot") in the tenth grade to continue their education there. As grade school boys, though, Jim and I had a lot of fun together. In fact, it was Jim who helped me to organize a schoolwide lunchroom strike in the seventh grade to demand better food. Organizing this strike was a perfectly normal thing for me, as the son of a textile mill executive whose business was built on nonunion labor, to do. Jim and I were both paddled by the school principal.

We are sometimes joined by one of my AA friends, Bill Monroe (not the country music singer). Bill is a retired physicist who had grown up in Tarboro, moved all over the country, then retired to Virginia Beach to live on a sailboat. He moved back to Tarboro after his house caught on fire and sank. Now he is occupied with restoring a 1956 Oldsmobile, and with something that he calls his, "little gravity project".

I particularly enjoy my conversations with Bill because science in general, and physics in particular, have played a huge role in my spiritual journey. There is a rich body of literature out there to support this path. Books with titles such as, *The Philosophical Impact of Contemporary Physics* and *The Elegant Universe*. Like the Universe, this body of work is expanding. Rather than conflicting with my faith, this material strengthens and expands it. These books proclaim the Kingdom of God by describing a Reality that is perfect to such a degree that it takes away doubt. They are modern affirmations of the perspective of the Upanishads –

> That is perfect. This is perfect. Perfect comes from perfect. Take perfect from perfect, the remainder is perfect.
>
> May peace and peace and peace be everywhere.

"Down to a sub-atomic level," Bill said. "If *anything* had been different, anything at all, we wouldn't be here."

"The Holocaust too?" I asked, already knowing the answer.

"Absolutely," he affirmed. "If all that hadn't happened, exactly as it did, we wouldn't be having this conversation. I might be here, because I was born before the Holocaust, but you would never have been born. Someone else might have shown up, but it would definitely not be you."

So, I thought. *Just like the life that I'm living today, which came out of the horrible drunken mess of my past, my very existence came out of that other, unimaginable horror. This path too, "takes away the sins of the world". It's true that "Jesus died for me", but so did Adolph Hitler.*

∞∞∞∞

There is a story, perhaps another legend, of an optional rearview mirror for Harley Davidson motorcycles. The inscription on the glass reads, "Assholes In The Mirror Are Closer Than They Appear". This is a wonderful meditation for me, since I know what my old teacher Sam Roundtree taught me is true. "There ain't nothing out there, but a reflection of me." When I judge my brother, I am *in fact* judging myself. It really does take one to know one.

Dianne and I live in our converted office building in downtown Tarboro. She walks to work at the Library most mornings. I keep house, go to Bible Study and Sunday school, do some AA work, and do some writing. We have a peaceful home. People like to come and see us. The tyrant king is not dead however. Civilizing him is the work of a lifetime.

Spinoza wrote that he could not admit that there is something positive in (so-called) sin. I most certainly can. Dianne and I would not be together today if it were not for my adultery in my first marriage and her husband's adultery in hers. Thank God for adultery!

People wound each other continuously "for we know not what we do". Imagine my surprise when I looked back at my life and found that nothing bad had ever happened to me. Nothing that happened to me happened apart from God's grace, and nothing *can* happen to me apart from that grace. I have a human life, and have no way of knowing what will happen when that comes to an end. I am incredibly grateful for the life that I've had, and if it turns out that I can have some influence on what happens next I would like to have another one, please. I have no desire to go to some never-ending heaven. Dianne says that she doesn't think anyone can make me go there.

My thinking today is really the same as it was in Mrs. Jenkins' 9th grade English class –

```
I have had a very exciting life and think
I wouldn't change a moment of it.
```

www.ingramcontent.com/pod-product-compliance
Lightning Source LLC
Chambersburg PA
CBHW020905100426
42737CB00043B/321